Conquering Third Grade

Reading
Mathematics
Science
Social Studies
Writing

Kristy Stark, M.A.Ed.

Publishing Credits

Corinne Burton, M.A.Ed., *President*; Conni Medina, M.A.Ed., *Managing Editor*; Emily R. Smith, M.A.Ed., *Content Director*; Lynette Ordoñez, *Editor*; Evan Ferrell, *Graphic Designer*; Lubabah Memon, *Assistant Editor*

Image Credits

pp. 19, 34, 62, 78, 142 Illustrations by Timothy J. Bradley; all other images from iStock and/or Shutterstock.

Standards

Shell Education
A division of Teacher Created Materials
5301 Oceanus Drive
Huntington Beach, CA 92649-1030

www.tcmpub.com/shell-education
ISBN 978-1-4258-1622-3

Table of Contents

Dear Family,

Welcome to *Conquering Third Grade*. Third grade will be an exciting and challenging year for your child. This book is designed to supplement the concepts your child is learning in third grade and to strengthen the connection between home and school. The activities in this book are based on today's standards and provide practice in reading, word study, language, writing, mathematics, social studies, and science. It also features fun, yet challenging, critical-thinking activities and games. In addition to the activity sheets in this book, the end of each section also provides engaging extension activities.

Your child should complete one unit per month, including the extension activities. This will allow your child to think about grade-level concepts over a longer period of time. This also ensures that the book can be completed in one school year.

Keep these tips in mind as you work with your child this year:

- Set aside specific times each week to work on the activities.
- Have your child complete one or two activities each time, rather than an entire unit at one time.
- Keep all practice sessions with your child positive and constructive. If the mood becomes tense or you and your child get frustrated, set the book aside and find another time to practice.
- Help your child with instructions, if necessary. If your child is having difficulty understanding what to do, work through some of the problems together.
- Encourage your child to do his or her best work, and compliment the effort that goes into learning.

Enjoy the time learning with your child during third grade. Summer will be here before you know it!

Sincerely,

The Shell Education Staff

Suggested Family Activities

Extend your child's learning by taking fun family field trips. A wide variety of experiences helps develop a child's vocabulary. Field trips also provide greater context and meaning to his or her learning in school.

A Trip to a Zoo

Bring a blank world map on a clipboard with you. As you visit each animal, have your child read the information placard and determine the original location of the animal or species. Then, have your child write the name of the animal on its continent on the map. At the end of your trip, determine which continent is home to the greatest number of animals at the zoo.

A Trip to a National Park

The National Park Service has a great program called Junior Rangers. If you go to a national park, check in with the rangers at the visitors center to see what tasks your child can complete to earn a Junior Ranger patch and/or certificate. Your child can also go to the WebRangers site (www.nps.gov/webrangers/) and check out a vacation spot, play games, and earn virtual rewards!

A Trip to a Museum

Before your trip, create a Bingo card of items you will find at the museum (for example, a mummy, a dinosaur bone, or an item made of clay). Make sure to leave space in each box for your child to write. As you navigate through the museum, have your child write one interesting fact about an item in its space on the card. When he or she gets four items in a row, celebrate the victory!

A Trip to a Farmers' Market

Turn a trip to your local farmers' market into a scavenger hunt by providing your child with a list of things to find. You could have him or her look for a vegetable that grows underground, a red fruit bigger than a fist, and so on. This is a great way for kids to discover different fruits, vegetables, and homemade items, as well as a chance to learn about farming and small businesses.

A Trip to a Library

Work with your child to find nonfiction books about an important person. First, ask your child whom he or she would like to learn more about. Your child can then use the digital catalog to search for books on this person that match his or her reading level. Then, your child can choose one or two nonfiction books about the person, check them out, and enjoy learning about someone's life!

Suggested Family Activities *(cont.)*

By discussing the activities in this book, you can enhance your child's learning. But it doesn't have to stop there. The suggestions below provide even more ideas on how to support your child's education.

General Skills

- Make sure your child gets plenty of exercise. Children need about 60 minutes of physical activity each day. You may want to have your child sign up for a sport. Or you can do fun things as a family, such as swimming, riding bicycles, or hiking.
- It's also important for children to get plenty of sleep. Children this age need between 9–11 hours of sleep each night. Establish a nightly bedtime routine that involves relaxing activities such as a warm shower or bath or reading a story.

Reading Skills

- Set a reading time for the entire family at least once every other day. Help your child choose a book at a comfortable reading level. Take turns reading aloud, one page at a time. Be sure to help him or her sound out and define unfamiliar words.
- Read books to your child that are above his or her reading level. This allows your child to experience more complex vocabulary, sentences, and ideas.

Writing Skills

- Set up a writing spot for your child. Have all of his or her writing materials in one special place. Having a designated area to write will help your child see writing as an important activity.
- Encourage your child to keep a daily journal or diary. Have your child spend 10 minutes a day writing about activities he or she did. The writing should also include his or her thoughts, feelings, likes and dislikes, and so on.

Mathematics Skills

- Have your child help you cook or bake. The kitchen is a great place to learn and practice fractions, multiplication, division, and other skills. Ask your child questions as you go along. For example: *If we only need to make half of the recipe, how many cups of flour will we need?*
- Include your child in grocery shopping. This is a great place to practice multiplication and division. Use the items in the store to help your child practice these skills.

Directions: Read the text, and answer the questions.

Ready to Fly

Sean was going on a plane to visit his uncle. It was the first time he had ever been on a plane alone. Sean was old enough to fly by himself. He knew which people to ask for help if he needed it. He had already met the flight attendants. His mom had packed a bag with games and snacks for the short flight. Sean smiled with satisfaction as he sat on the plane by himself. He was ready to go!

1. What is the text about?
   - (A) a plane carrying only one passenger
   - (B) a child traveling alone on a plane to visit family
   - (C) feeling lonely on an airplane trip
   - (D) a passenger wanting to be left alone on a plane

2. What is the setting?
   - (A) Sean's house
   - (B) a park
   - (C) a grocery store
   - (D) an airport

3. Which word has the same blend as *plane*?
   - (A) upload
   - (B) apple
   - (C) plate
   - (D) uncle

4. What is the definition of *attendants*?
   - (A) servants
   - (B) workers who serve or help
   - (C) people who sell tickets
   - (D) people who fly planes

5. Which is a synonym for *satisfaction*?
   - (A) happiness
   - (B) sadness
   - (C) loneliness
   - (D) grumpiness

6. Which new title best fits the text?
   - (A) "All About Airplanes"
   - (B) "Sean Learns to Fly"
   - (C) "Sean's First Solo Flight"
   - (D) "Sean Is Bored"

Directions: Read the text, and answer the questions.

The Trouble with Pollution

Pollution on the beach is troubling. Some of that trash comes from people at the beach. Throwing garbage on the sand pollutes the water because the trash makes its way into the ocean. Some of the trash washes up on the beach from the ocean. Pollution can come from many places. People can work together to clean up the beach. It makes the beach a nicer place to visit. It helps wildlife there, too!

1. Which type of image would tell a reader more about this text?
   - (A) a list of wildlife found on the beach
   - (B) a photograph of a fishing boat
   - (C) a photograph of a polluted beach
   - (D) a picture of a "No Swimming" sign

2. Which word from the text makes a new word by adding the prefix *re-*?
   - (A) visit
   - (B) place
   - (C) makes
   - (D) all of the above

3. Which of these words is the root word of *pollution*?
   - (A) revolution
   - (B) pollute
   - (C) poll
   - (D) Polly

4. Based on the text, which statement is true?
   - (A) The author wants to teach people about keeping beaches clean.
   - (B) The author thinks all beaches are filthy.
   - (C) The author compares air pollution and water pollution.
   - (D) The author uses facts to tell the history of pollution.

Directions: Write each spelling word in print and in cursive.

Aa	Bb	Cc	Dd	Ee	Ff	Gg	Hh	Ii	Jj	Kk	Ll	Mm
Nn	Oo	Pp	Qq	Rr	Ss	Tt	Uu	Vv	Ww	Xx	Yy	Zz

1. afraid
2. because
3. brought
4. everything
5. morning
6. people
7. though
8. twenty
9. window
10. yesterday

UNIT 1

Language

Directions: Answer each question.

1. Add quotation marks to the sentence.

The dog has not been fed yet, my mother told us.

2. Add a comma to the sentence.

Frank yelled "We are the state champions!"

3. Add a comma to the following address.

1700 Lakeview Place
Springfield OR 99810

4. Rewrite the book title *the zookeeper's job* using correct capitalization.

____

5. Write your address. Be sure to use commas correctly.

____

____

6. Rewrite the song title "bicycle built for two" using correct capitalization.

____

Directions: Place check marks in the circles with information that you would include in an informative/explanatory paragraph about animals in the tundra.

Tundra Animal Facts

- These animals either hibernate or migrate for the winter.
- They have minimal skin exposure to stay warm.
- The largest tundra animal is the polar bear.
- They have adaptations for survival.
- There are about 48 different animals in the tundra.
- Polar bear cubs are cute.

Directions: Write a paragraph describing the types of animals that live in a tundra. Include specific facts about how the animals adapt and live in the environment. Use the facts on page 11 to help you.

Remember!

A strong informative/explanatory paragraph should include:

- a topic sentence
- details to support the main idea
- a concluding sentence

Directions: Solve each problem.

UNIT 1

Mathematics

1. $\begin{array}{r} 5 \\ \times \ 2 \\ \hline \end{array}$ ☐

5. $\begin{array}{r} 3 \\ \times \ 5 \\ \hline \end{array}$ ☐

2. $9 \times 5 =$ ☐

6. $7 \times 4 =$ ☐

3. $\begin{array}{r} 7 \\ \times \ 7 \\ \hline \end{array}$ ☐

7. $\begin{array}{r} 9 \\ \times \ 3 \\ \hline \end{array}$ ☐

4. $\begin{array}{r} 10 \\ \times \ 6 \\ \hline \end{array}$ ☐

8. $\begin{array}{r} 8 \\ \times \ 4 \\ \hline \end{array}$ ☐

Directions: Solve each problem.

1. $\begin{array}{r} 20 \\ -\ 15 \\ \hline \end{array}$ ☐

2. 16 + 3 = ______________

3. $\begin{array}{r} 25 \\ -\ 10 \\ \hline \end{array}$ ☐

4. 48 − 24 = ☐

5. $\begin{array}{r} 62 \\ -\ 37 \\ \hline \end{array}$ ☐

6. 34 − 12 = ______________

7. $\begin{array}{r} 54 \\ +\ 25 \\ \hline \end{array}$ ☐

8. 50 − 36 = ☐

9.  +  = ______________

Directions: Look at the examples. Then, solve the problems.

Example: Label 472 on the number line.

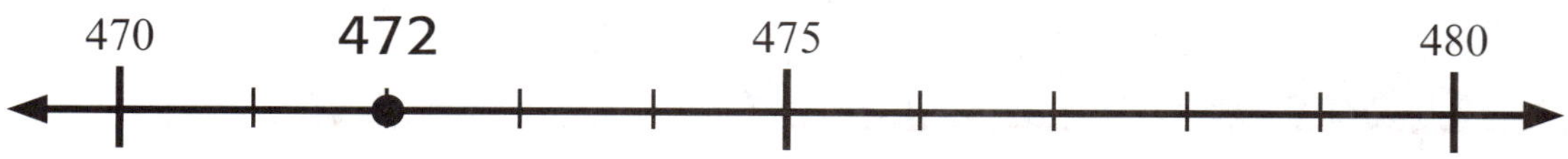

Round 472 to the nearest ten. 470

Example: Label 472 on the number line.

Round 472 to the nearest hundred. 500

1. Label 617 on the number line

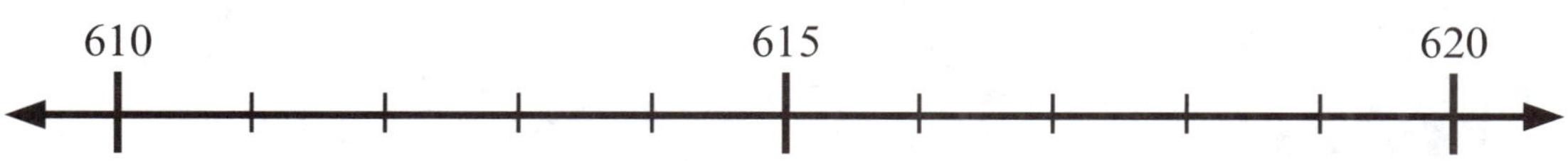

Round 617 to the nearest ten. ____________________

2. Label 617 on the number line.

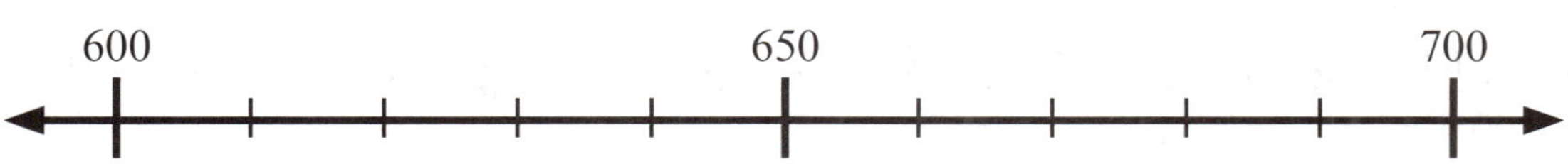

Round 617 to the nearest hundred. ________________

Directions: Show two ways to solve the problem.

1. Lucy is thinking of a number. When she rounds her number to the nearest ten, it is 200. What number might Lucy be thinking of? Find as many solutions as possible.

Strategy 1

Use a number line to find the solutions.

Strategy 2

Show a different strategy to find the solutions.

2. Which strategy do you think is easier? Explain your reasoning.

____

____

____

Directions: Imagine that you are in charge of your school. List the rules you would make to keep students safe. Then, answer the questions.

- ____
- ____
- ____
- ____
- ____

1. How are your rules similar to the rules your school already has?

2. What rules did you write that your school does not already have? Why do you think they are important?

Directions: Follow the steps in this experiment to discover what happens to cold containers.

What You Need

- ice cubes
- small container with lid

What to Do

1. Put as many ice cubes as you can into the container. Seal the container.
2. Describe the outside of the container.

   ____

   ____

3. Leave the container alone for half an hour. Then, observe the outside of the container again. Describe it.

   ____

   ____

4. On a separate sheet of paper, draw and label a diagram of what happened.
5. What do you think happened? Where did the water come from?

   ____

   ____

   ____

   ____

Directions: Look at each puzzle. Write the word or phase that each puzzle represents.

1. playing s i d e

____

2. SECRET
SECRET
SECRET
SECRET

____

3. H
I
L
L

____

4. eggs
―――
easy

____

5. AID AID AID

____

6. looking

____

Directions: Work with a partner. Take turns rolling two number cubes. Write the two numbers you rolled. Then, multiply the numbers and write the answer. Use the example below to help you. The person with the highest product wins.

 ×  = 8

1. ____________________

2. ____________________

3. ____________________

4. ____________________

5. ____________________

6. ____________________

7. ____________________

8. ____________________

9. ____________________

10. ____________________

Spelling Activity

Write a funny story that uses all the spelling words on page 9.

Writing Activity

Research a type of biome other than the tundra. Write an informative/explanatory paragraph about the animals that live there.

Mathematics Activity

Choose one multiplication problem from page 13. Use small objects or draw a picture to prove that your answer is correct.

Problem-Solving Activity

Ask a family member to write 10 three-digit numbers. Round each one to the nearest ten and the nearest hundred.

Social Studies Activity

With your family, create a list of rules for your home. Post the rules in a place where everyone can see them.

Critical-Thinking Activity

Create your own puzzles like those on page 19. See if someone can solve your puzzles.

Directions: Read the text, and answer the questions.

Joshua's Rides

Joshua rides his bike to work each day, rain or shine. He wears special waterproof gear so that he stays dry on rainy or foggy mornings. He believes that riding a bike is a great way to start the day. The ride home gives him time to think and reflect on his day. The roads are usually quiet. It makes him wonder why more people are not riding bikes each day.

1. Which new title best fits the text?
   - (A) "Biking to Work"
   - (B) "Biking, Rain or Shine"
   - (C) "A Biking Fool"
   - (D) "Reflecting"
2. Why does Joshua enjoy riding his bike?
   - (A) He can reflect on his day.
   - (B) He can enjoy the quiet roads.
   - (C) It gives him time to think.
   - (D) all of the above
3. Which word has the same root word as *riding*?
   - (A) rid
   - (B) rider
   - (C) side
   - (D) decide
4. Which words in the text are synonyms?
   - (A) *wonder* and *reflect*
   - (B) *rides* and *wear*
   - (C) *day* and *morning*
   - (D) *think* and *quiet*
5. What does *rain or shine* mean?
   - (A) raining very hard
   - (B) warm rain
   - (C) no matter what the weather is
   - (D) drying off after a lot of rain
6. Which word best describes Joshua?
   - (A) lazy
   - (B) reflective
   - (C) boring
   - (D) curious

Directions: Read the text, and answer the questions.

Sir Edmund and Mount Everest

Sir Edmund Hillary was an amazing man. He was one of the first people to reach the top of Mount Everest. This is the tallest mountain in the world. His group reached the peak in 1953. Hillary was curious about this part of the world. He returned to the region after his climb. He raised funds for small towns near the mountain. This money helped people build bridges, schools, and hospitals. He worked hard to make the world a better place.

1. Which image would tell a reader more about this text?
   - (A) a photograph of a school
   - (B) a picture of money used in this part of the world
   - (C) a photograph of a home
   - (D) a photograph of Sir Edmund Hillary

2. Which new title best reflects the main idea?
   - (A) "Up to the Peak"
   - (B) "The Amazing Sir Edmund"
   - (C) "Building Bridges"
   - (D) "Parts of the World"

3. What is the definition of *funds* as it is used in this text?
   - (A) supplies
   - (B) accounts
   - (C) treasures
   - (D) money

4. What is the author's opinion of Sir Edmund Hillary?
   - (A) The author doubts his achievements.
   - (B) The author respects him.
   - (C) The author does not understand him.
   - (D) The author is confused by him.

UNIT 2

Spelling

Directions: Write the two words that make up each spelling word. Then, write what each spelling word means.

Word	Two Words	Meaning
1 afternoon	________ + ________	
2 airplane	________ + ________	
3 anything	________ + ________	
4 backyard	________ + ________	
5 birthday	________ + ________	
6 hairbrush	________ + ________	
7 staircase	________ + ________	
8 something	________ + ________	
9 sometime	________ + ________	
10 toothbrush	________ + ________	

Directions: Answer each question.

1. Circle the adverb in the sentence.

   Nina walked home quickly to make it in time for her favorite show.

2. Write the correct verb to complete the sentence.

   When my teacher got angry with me, I ________________ embarrassed.
   (*felt, feel, feelings*)

3. Rewrite the sentence in the future tense.

   I walk to school every day.

   ____

4. An abstract noun is a noun that cannot be identified using the five senses. Circle the abstract noun in the sentence.

   I have some knowledge about the rules of tennis.

5. Write the correct adverb to complete the sentence.

   I mow the lawn ________________________ than my brother.
   (*often, more often, most often*)

6. Write a sentence using the noun *childhood*.

   ____

   ____

Directions: Draw a winter scene and a spring scene. Write two opinions about each season.

Winter

____

____

____

Spring

____

____

____

Directions: It's a contest! Winter and spring both think they're the better season. Write a paragraph about which season you prefer. Provide reasons to support your opinion. Use your notes from page 26 to help you.

Remember!

A strong opinion paragraph:

- has an introductory and a concluding sentence stating an opinion
- gives reasons that support the opinion

Directions: Solve each problem.

1. How many rows of 2 make 14?

____

2. Is this an equal share?

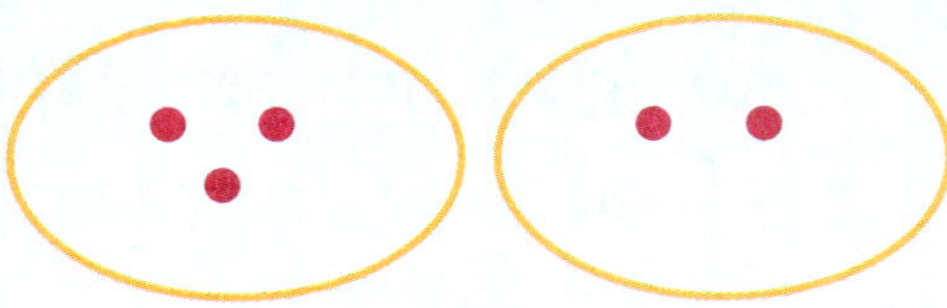

Circle: yes no

3. How many groups of 4 are in 16?

____

4. How many lines of 5 make 30?

____

5. Use different colors to show four equal groups.

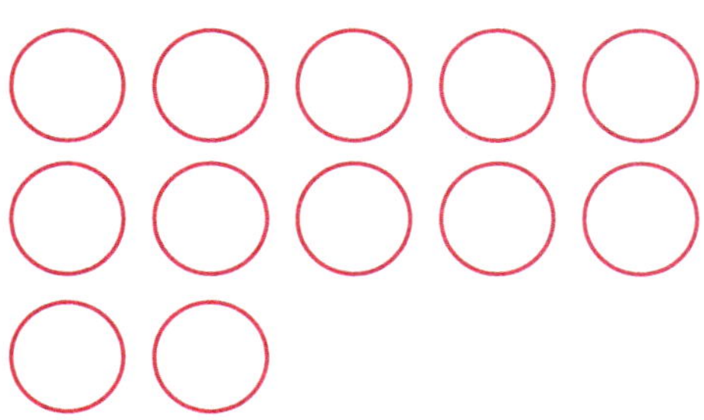

6. How many rows of 2 make 10?

____

7. Circle groups of 2.

8. How many rows of 2 make 18?

____

9. How many rows of 5 make 35?

____

10. How many groups of 7 make 42?

____

Directions: Solve each problem.

1. Write the time in words.

2. What time is shown?

3. Show 12 o'clock on the clock.

4. Show 10:15 on the clock.

5. Write the time in words.

6. What time is shown?

7. Write the time in words.

8. Show half past 2:00 on the clock.

Directions: Look at the example. Then, solve the problem using the number line.

Example: 153 + 129 = ☐

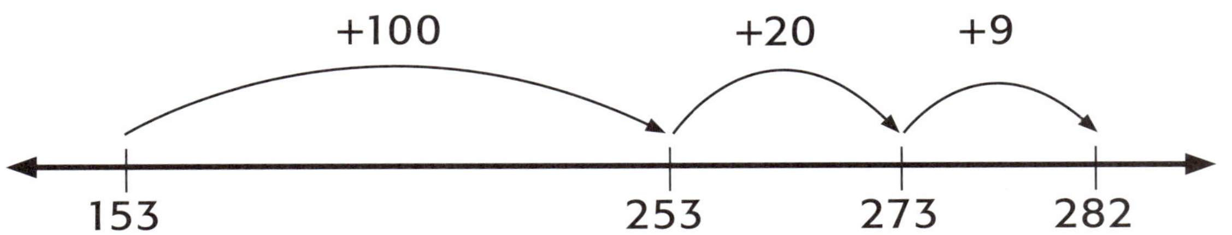

153 + 100 + 20 + 9 = 282

153 + 129 = 282

235 + 164 = ☐

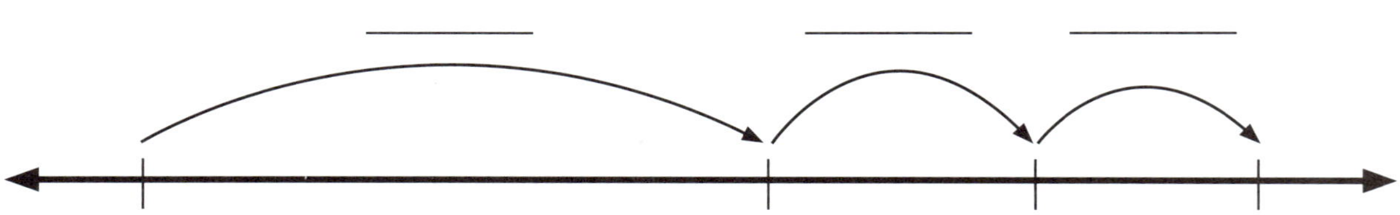

________ + ________ + ________ + ________ = ________

235 + 164 = ______

Directions: Show two ways to solve the problem.

1. Find the missing number.

$355 + 150 = \square + 275$

Strategy 1

Strategy 2

2. Which strategy do you think is better? Explain your reasoning.

UNIT 2

Social Studies

Directions: Read the definition of the word *volunteer*. Then, answer the questions.

volunteer: a person who offers his or her time without being paid

1. How can you volunteer at home?

____

____

____

2. How can you volunteer in your community?

____

____

____

3. Why is volunteering important?

____

____

____

____

____

Directions: Follow the steps in this experiment to discover what soil is made of.

What You Need

- soil sample
- graduated sieves
- containers

What to Do

1. Collect a small sample of soil. It should be about 250 grams (8 oz.).
2. Sift the soil through the largest sieve. Place whatever does not fit through the sieve into a container.
3. Sift the rest of the soil through the next sieve. Place what does not fit in another container. Continue in this way from the largest to the smallest sieve.
4. Record what is in each container. Describe the size of the materials, their colors, and their textures.

Sieve 1	Sieve 2	Sieve 3	Sieve 4

5. What can you conclude about your soil sample?

____

____

Directions: Look at each picture. Write the word each picture represents. Circle *ice* in each word.

1

____

4

____

2

____

5

____

3

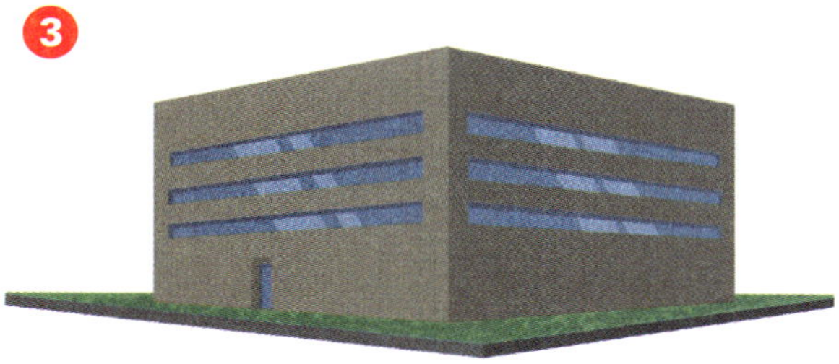

____

6

____

Directions: Play with a partner. Take turns rolling two number cubes. Match your roll to a word in the chart. Write that word in your Word Bank. After your second turn, see if you can make a compound word out of the words in your Word Bank. If you can, write it on one of the lines. The first player to write three compound words wins.

2	3	4	5	6	7
any	birth	brush	case	day	hair

8	9	10	11	12
some	stair	thing	time	tooth

Player 1: ____________	Player 2: ____________
Word Bank	**Word Bank**

____________ ____________

____________ ____________

____________ ____________

Spelling Activity

Create a list of compound words. Add to the list as you read more compound words.

Writing Activity

What is your favorite way to volunteer? Why? Write a paragraph to support your opinion.

Mathematics Activity

Write a schedule of your day. Include the times when you usually do things throughout the day.

Problem-Solving Activity

Write the numbers 0–9 on separate slips of paper. Place them in a bag, and randomly choose three slips. Use them to create a 3-digit number. Pull three more numbers out of the bag to create a second 3-digit number. Use two strategies to add them.

Science Activity

Collect a soil sample from another location, and repeat the experiment. Compare your results to the original experiment from page 33. How are the two samples alike and different?

Listening-and-Speaking Activity

Ask your family members about ways you can volunteer at home. Summarize their suggestions in your own words. Then, choose one of their suggestions, and help out at home.

Directions: Read the text, and answer the questions.

Planning a Party

"Planning a birthday party is hard," thought Jenna. She could not pick which friends to invite. Jenna was having a slumber party, so her parents thought she should only have a few guests. It was hard to narrow down her list. Jenna had friends at school and from her soccer team. She had friends from summer camp, too. She did not know how to include everyone in one event.

1. Which word or phrase tells the reader the most about this text?
   - (A) summer
   - (B) friends
   - (C) slumber party
   - (D) soccer

2. Which new title best describes the main idea?
   - (A) "Making a List"
   - (B) "A Hard Choice"
   - (C) "Jenna's Day"
   - (D) "A Great Party"

3. Which word has the same vowel sound as *have*?
   - (A) happy
   - (B) haze
   - (C) frame
   - (D) paid

4. Which sentence best describes this text?
   - (A) The text describes a funny situation.
   - (B) The text details an event.
   - (C) The text describes a problem.
   - (D) The text lists steps in a certain order.

5. What word best describes how Jenna is feeling?
   - (A) happy
   - (B) stubborn
   - (C) confused
   - (D) sad

Reading

Directions: Read the text, and answer the questions.

A Good Way to Stay Healthy

One way to stay healthy is to get enough vitamins. Vitamins are found in healthy foods. They help our bodies work well. It is always best to get vitamins from food. But it can be hard to get enough from food alone. A pill can also be taken. It has nutrients inside. A vitamin a day can keep the doctor away.

1. Which word best summarizes this text?
   - (A) vitamins
   - (B) doctor
   - (C) foods
   - (D) inside

2. What is the main idea of the text?
   - (A) Vitamins are only found in food.
   - (B) Vitamins help you stay healthy.
   - (C) Doctors want you to take vitamins.
   - (D) Vitamins are only for adults.

3. Which word has a vowel sound like the word *pill*?
   - (A) krill
   - (B) dial
   - (C) height
   - (D) bull

4. Which word is the antonym of *away*?
   - (A) inside
   - (B) here
   - (C) stay
   - (D) taken

5. *A vitamin a day can keep the doctor away* is closely related to which popular saying?
   - (A) It's raining cats and dogs.
   - (B) Another day, another dollar.
   - (C) She is in hot water.
   - (D) An apple a day keeps the doctor away.

Directions: Look at each pair of words in the first chart. Decide how the first word was changed before adding *–ing*. Write either *no change*, *drop the e*, or *double the consonant*. In the second chart, write the word with *–ing*, and then write how you changed it.

Word	Word with *–ing*	Change
1 believe	believing	
2 have	having	
3 read	reading	
4 run	running	
5 decide	deciding	

Word	Word with *–ing*	Change
6 sit		
7 depend		
8 make		
9 forget		
10 take		

Directions: Circle the word in each set that is spelled correctly.

1	lateley	latly	lately
2	really	realy	realley
3	briteness	brightness	brightniss
4	finding	fynding	findeing
5	bushs	bushs'	bushes
6	benches	benchs	benchus
7	cryes	crys	cries
8	droppt	droped	dropped
9	diveing	diving	dyving
10	happely	happyly	happily

Directions: Think about a time you celebrated a holiday. Write the name of the holiday in the center circle. Then, write notes about the event in the outer circles. Be sure to include whom you celebrated with and what happened.

My Holiday Celebration

Directions: Think about a holiday you have celebrated. Write a narrative describing the celebration. Include at least two lines of dialogue. Use your notes on page 41 to help you.

Remember!

A strong narrative paragraph:

- includes an introductory and a concluding sentence
- uses sensory details to describe the experience
- makes it sound like a story

Directions: Solve each problem.

1. $8 + 8 = \square + 4$

2. $15 - \square = 6 + 2$

3. Write the missing number.

   24, 28, ________, 36, 40

4. $5 + 5 + 5 + 5 = \square \times 5$

5. $15 \bigcirc 3 = 12$

6. $3 \times 4 = 4 + 4 + \square$

7. $14 - \square = 8 + 5$

8. Write the next 3 numbers in the pattern.

   250, 200, 150, ________, ________, ________

Directions: Solve each problem.

1. What smaller shapes were used to make the large rectangle?

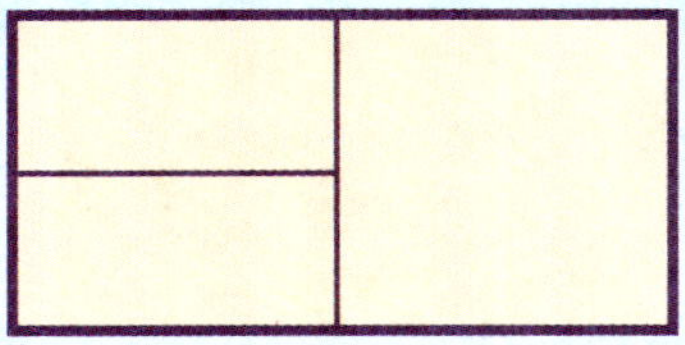

____

2. Name the solid shape.

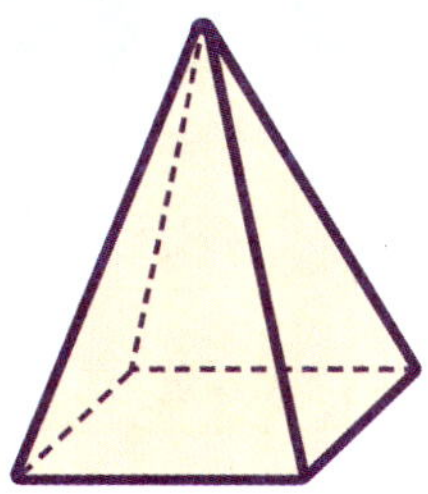

____

3. Draw the top view.

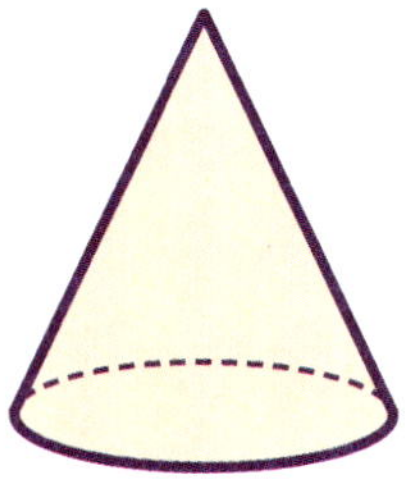

4. Name the solid shape.

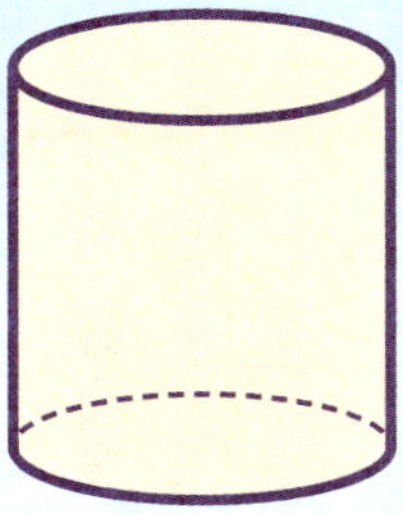

____

5. Does the arrow point to a face, a vertex, or an edge?

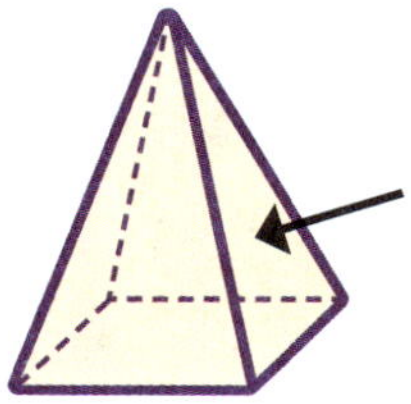

____

6. Draw the top view.

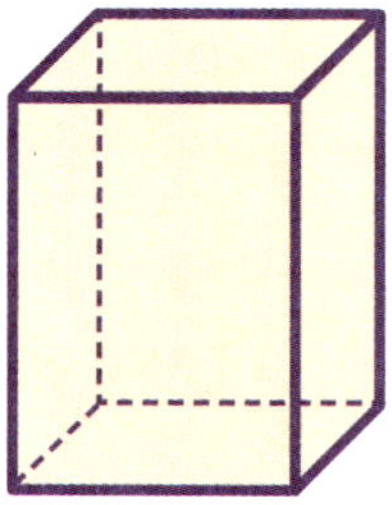

Directions: Look at the example. Then, solve the problem using the number line.

Example: 618 − 397 = ☐

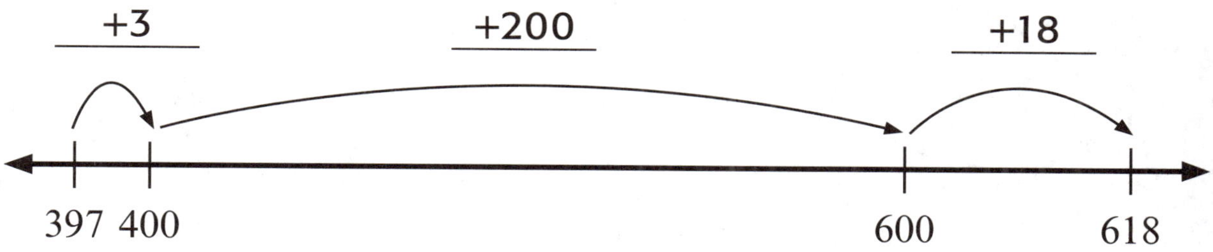

3 + 200 + 18 = 221

618 − 397 = 221

562 − 279 = ☐

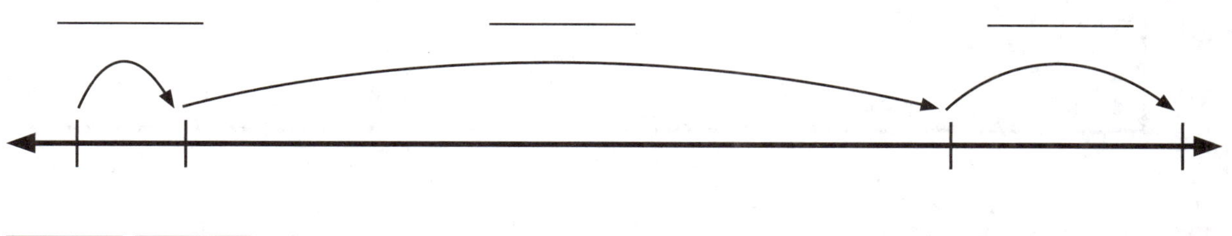

_____ + _____ + _____ = _____

562 − 279 = _____

Directions: Show two ways to solve the problem.

1. On Monday, a flower shop had 740 roses. By Saturday, there were 329 roses left. How many roses did the flower shop sell?

Strategy 1

Strategy 2

2. Which strategy do you like better? Explain your reasoning.

____

____

____

Directions: Study the terms in the Word Bank. Look up any terms you don't know. Then, write the terms in the correct columns to show if the person or group makes or enforces rules. Some terms may appear in both columns.

Word Bank

- city council
- parking enforcement
- principal
- teacher
- Congress
- police officer
- security guard

Makes Rules	Enforces Rules

UNIT 3

Science

Directions: Follow the steps in this experiment to discover when the sun rises and sets.

What You Need

5 consecutive days of your local weather forecast

What to Do

1. Look at your local weather forecast. You can find this in a newspaper, or you can ask an adult to help you find it online. Record the time of sunrise and sunset each day.

Date	Sunrise	Sunset

2. What season is it right now?

____

3. What do you notice about the sunrise and sunset times?

____

____

____

____

Directions: Solve each riddle.

1. I am a number between 80 and 100. If you divide me by 3, you get 30. What am I?

2. I am a number between 50 and 60. I have 4 ones. What am I?

3. I am an odd number. If you multiply me by myself, you get 49. What am I?

4. I am an even number. I am greater than 35 but less than 38. What am I?

5. I am a number equal to the number of cents in one quarter, one dime, and 3 pennies. What am I?

6. I am an odd number. If you add 49 to me, you get 124. What am I?

Directions: Work with a partner. Take turns rolling a number cube. Match your roll to one of the shapes in the chart. Draw this shape in the space below the chart. Use the shapes you draw to make a funny picture. Roll at least 10 times.

Shapes

Spelling Activity

Write the spelling words from page 39 in your best cursive handwriting.

Writing Activity

Make up a fictional holiday. Write a narrative about you celebrating this holiday with your friends and family.

Mathematics Activity

Look for shapes in the world around you. Keep track of the shapes you see, and make a chart to show which shapes you see more than the others. Challenge yourself to make a graph with the data you collected.

Science Activity

Ask an adult to help you look up the sunrise and sunset times in your area for different seasons. What do you notice?

Critical-Thinking Activity

Write your own number riddles like those on page 49. See if someone can solve your riddles.

Listening-and-Speaking Activity

Interview a person in your home who makes the rules for your family. Ask him or her to explain why those rules were made and how he or she enforces them.

Directions: Read the text, and answer the questions.

Joe's Exercise

Joe was not a competitive person. He did not like to win or lose. He really did not like to compete against anyone for anything. For this reason, Joe didn't enjoy playing most sports. He thought it was a waste of time to play with a team. Yet, he still liked to move his body and exercise. One day, Joe decided to start swimming. He thought it would be a peaceful way to exercise. It was just Joe in the water, and there was no competition. Joe decided that he loved swimming! He vowed to go swimming as often as he could.

1. Which question about the text would help readers monitor their reading?
   - (A) How do you swim?
   - (B) How do you play football?
   - (C) How does Joe exercise?
   - (D) Where are swim lessons?

2. Which of these words has the same root word as *swimming*?
   - (A) swish
   - (B) timing
   - (C) winning
   - (D) swimmer

3. Which simile describes Joe's experience while swimming?
   - (A) smart as a whip
   - (B) quiet as a mouse
   - (C) surprising like a shooting star
   - (D) loud as a firecracker

4. What type of text is this?
   - (A) persuasive
   - (B) narrative
   - (C) fantasy
   - (D) fairy tale

Directions: Read the text, and answer the questions.

Snowboarding

Snowboarders like to take risks. They enjoy the thrill of a fun ride on the snow. Many fans of the sport like to snowboard in a half-pipe, which is a U-shaped bowl. Riders can move from one side of the bowl to the other. They jump and do tricks inside the half-pipe. The half-pipe started with skateboarders. Now, snowboarders enjoy it. It takes a lot of practice to do some snowboarding tricks, but it sure is fun!

1. What does the first sentence tell about this text?
   - (A) The text is about snowboarders.
   - (B) The text is about going for a ride.
   - (C) The text is about safety in the snow.
   - (D) The text is about a risk.

2. Which chapter title would help a reader find this information in a table of contents?
   - (A) "Doing Tricks"
   - (B) "The Thrill of Snowboarding"
   - (C) "Jump and Spin"
   - (D) "A Fun Day"

3. Which of the following is a synonym for *risks*?
   - (A) choices
   - (B) dangers
   - (C) gears
   - (D) speeds

4. What type of text is most similar to this text?
   - (A) a story about sports
   - (B) a book of poetry
   - (C) a list of directions
   - (D) a math textbook

5. Which phrase from the text is an opinion?
   - (A) they jump and do tricks
   - (B) it takes a lot of practice
   - (C) it sure is fun
   - (D) riders can move from one side of the bowl to the other

Directions: Write each word. Then, write each word backward.

1. above ______________ ______________

2. always ______________ ______________

3. bought ______________ ______________

4. himself ______________ ______________

5. month ______________ ______________

6. should ______________ ______________

7. stopped ______________ ______________

8. teacher ______________ ______________

9. weather ______________ ______________

10. without ______________ ______________

Directions: Answer each question.

1. What does the adjective *blue* describe in the sentence?

   When I look at the gorgeous ocean, all I can see is the clear, blue water.

   ____

2. Rewrite the sentence using the correct pronoun.

   My sister never wants to share his toys with me.

   ____

   ____

3. Circle the adjectives in the sentence.

   The brown horse galloped along the sandy beach.

4. Circle the plural noun in the sentence.

   People visited the zoo today.

5. Circle the proper noun.

   Where should Mary go to walk her dog on a trail?

6. Write the correct adjective to complete the sentence

   Mom was ____________________ than Dad at the mess.
   (*angry*, *angrier*, *angriest*)

Directions: Read the statements about earthquakes. Write *F* if the statement is a fact. Write *O* if the statement is an opinion.

1. ______ About 50,000 earthquakes happen every year.
2. ______ I get scared during earthquakes.
3. ______ It's important to have a safety plan for when an earthquake hits.
4. ______ Most earthquakes go unnoticed.
5. ______ Sometimes, aftershocks happen after a big earthquake hits.
6. ______ Scientists measure the magnitude of earthquakes with seismometers.
7. ______ People prefer to have earthquakes at night.
8. ______ Earth's moving plates are what cause earthquakes.

Directions: Write an informative/explanatory paragraph about earthquakes. Include facts about how they begin and what destruction they can cause. Use the facts from page 56 to help you.

Remember!

Your informative/explanatory paragraph should include:

- a topic sentence
- details to support the main idea
- a concluding sentence

Directions: Solve each problem.

1. $\$1.32 + \$2.45$

2. What is the total value of these coins?

____

3. True or false?
100 pennies = 3 quarters

____

4. $0.35 + $0.25 = ______________________

5. $0.15 + $0.25 + $0.10 = ______________________

6. $\$5.45 + \$3.25$

7. $\$1.79 + \$2.52$

8. True or false?
1 half dollar = 2 quarters

____

9. $1.15 + $0.42 + $1.02 = ______________________

10. How many nickels are there in $1.20?

____

UNIT 4

Mathematics

Directions: Solve each problem.

1. $\begin{array}{r} 10 \\ \times \; 8 \\ \hline \end{array}$ ☐

2. What is 10 times 0? ______

3. 10 × 10 = ______.

4. 40 × 8 = ☐

5. $\begin{array}{r} 10 \\ \times \; 3 \\ \hline \end{array}$ ☐

6. $\begin{array}{r} 20 \\ \times \; 8 \\ \hline \end{array}$ ☐

7. What is 2 times 10? ______

8. 10 × 7 = ☐

9. 30 × 3 = ☐

10. $\begin{array}{r} 50 \\ \times \; 6 \\ \hline \end{array}$ ☐

Directions: Read and solve each problem.

Problem 1: Shawn has 65 crayons. He gives some to his sister. He has 38 crayons left. How many crayons did Shawn give to his sister?

List What You Know	Make a Plan
Solve the Problem	**Look Back and Explain**

Problem 2: Kevin has many comic books. He gave away 14 old books. He has 62 comic books left. How many books did he start with?

List What You Know	Make a Plan
Solve the Problem	**Look Back and Explain**

Directions: Show two ways to solve the problem.

1. A bus picked up 32 people at the first stop. At the second stop, 12 people got off. At the next stop, 6 more people got off, but 10 got on. How many passengers are on the bus now?

Strategy 1

Strategy 2

2. Which strategy do you think is better? Explain your reasoning.

Directions: Imagine you are in charge of your city. Answer the questions below to show how you would run the city.

1. Who would help you run the city? Why?

____

____

____

2. What laws would you make?

____

____

____

3. Why are these laws important?

____

____

____

4. How would you keep people safe?

____

____

____

Directions: Follow the steps in this experiment to discover how plants grow.

What You Need

- paper towels
- 4 plastic cups
- ruler
- water
- measuring spoon
- 4 types of beans (from seed packets)

What to Do

1. Put a paper towel in the bottom of each plastic cup.
2. Pour 15 mL (3 tsp) of water into the bottom of each cup so that the paper towel is damp. Number the cups from 1 to 4.
3. In each cup, put a different type of bean seed on top of the paper towel. Cover each with another damp paper towel.
4. Place the cups on a windowsill. Water them each day for two weeks. Measure and record the plants' growth each day on a separate sheet of paper.
5. Which bean sprouted first? Which bean sprouted last?

____

____

6. Why do you think you got these results?

____

____

Directions: Find how many total squares are in this picture.

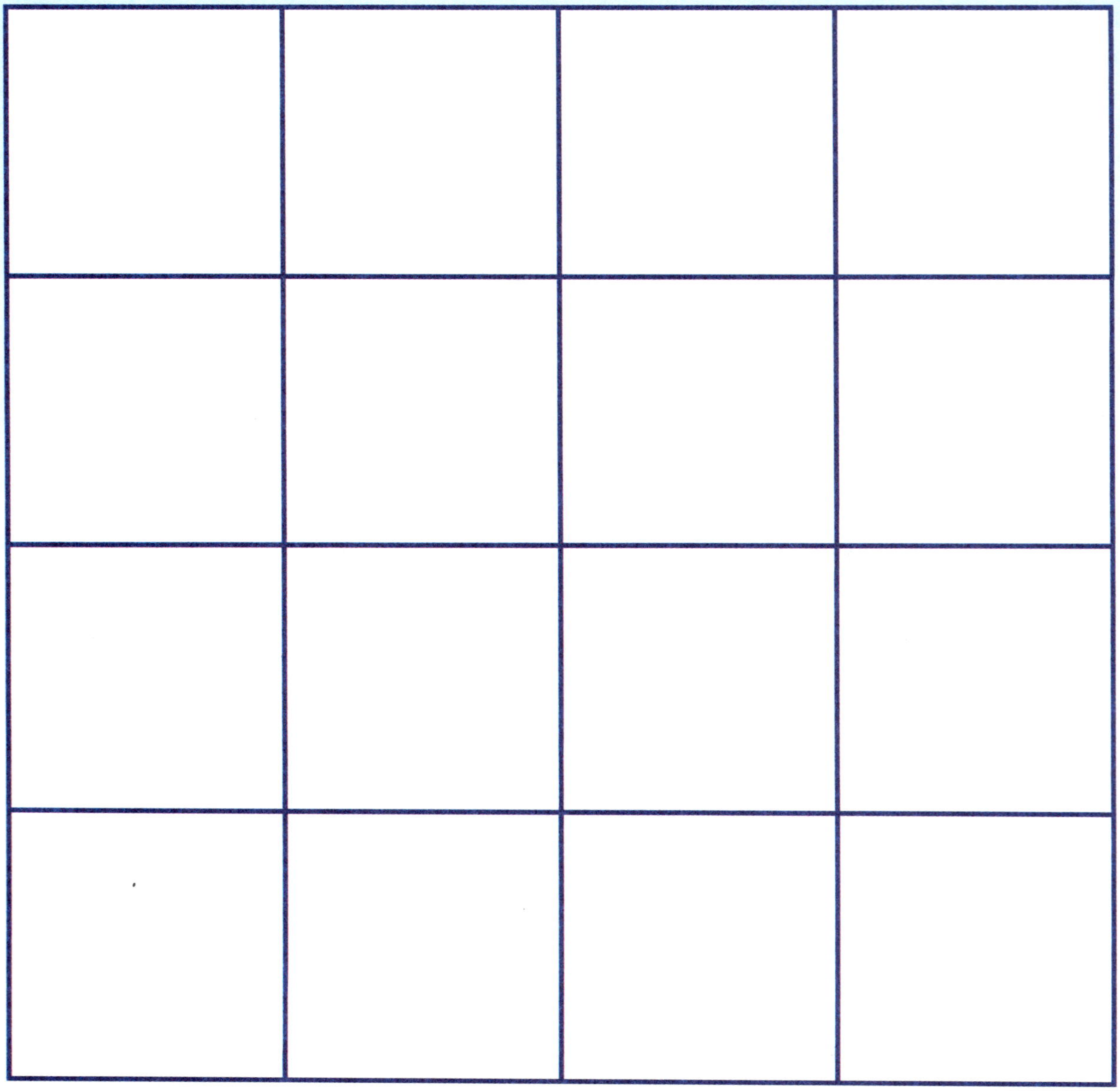

________________ total squares

Directions: Work with a partner. Take turns rolling a number cube two times per turn. The first roll tells you which column to look at. The second roll tells you which row. Read the word in the column and row number that you rolled. For example, if you roll a 6 and then a 2, you would read the word *paint*. Cross out each word you read. Continue until all the squares are crossed out.

	student	cried	friend	imagine	tried	shadow
	explain	speak	tomorrow	flower	school	paint
	house	road	question	balloon	bounce	piece
	know	window	mountain	looked	watched	perfect
	above	always	bought	himself	month	should
	stopped	teacher	weather	without	believe	have

Spelling Activity

Write silly sentences with the spelling words on page 54 in your best cursive handwriting.

Mathematics Activity

Choose five one-digit numbers. Multiply each of those numbers by 10. Then, multiply each number by a different one-digit number.

Science Activity

Repeat the experiment on page 63 with a different type of plant. Compare and contrast how the plant grows to how the bean plants grew.

Social Studies Activity

Ask a family member what city laws he or she thinks are important. Add those to your plan on page 62.

Critical-Thinking Activity

Draw a large rectangle. Divide it so that there are smaller rectangles or squares inside it. Then, see how many rectangles you can count.

Listening-and-Speaking Activity

Talk with your family about natural disasters that occur in your area. Discuss what you should do in case of a natural disaster. Then, make an emergency plan with your family.

Directions: Read the text, and answer the questions.

Anna was having a hard year because she did not have many friends in her class. She wasn't sure why, since she knew that kids liked her, but she really wanted a best friend. "Will you be my best friend?" she asked Pamela one day.

"What about Nina or Sara?" Pamela asked. "They tell everyone that they are your best friends. But they say that you never play with them." Anna saw the problem immediately. She was so busy looking for a best friend that she forgot to be a good friend to Nina and Sara.

1. Which word tells a reader more about this text while previewing it?
   - (A) kids
   - (B) busy
   - (C) friends
   - (D) play

2. Which title best describes the main idea of this text?
   - (A) "Anna and Pamela"
   - (B) "Finding Friends"
   - (C) "Talking to Friends"
   - (D) "An Awful Day"

3. What word part could you add to the root *miss* and make a new word?
   - (A) *-er*
   - (B) *-ly*
   - (C) *dis-*
   - (D) *un-*

4. Which word or phrase is an antonym for *immediately*?
   - (A) closely
   - (B) at once
   - (C) later
   - (D) never

5. The language in the text is best described as
   - (A) persuasive.
   - (B) formal.
   - (C) technical.
   - (D) informal.

6. What do you think Anna will do next?
   - (A) continue looking for a best friend
   - (B) become best friends with Pamela
   - (C) play with Nina and Sara
   - (D) become best friends with someone in her class

Directions: Read the text, and answer the questions.

Rip Currents

Swimming in the ocean is fun. But it can be dangerous, too. A riptide can pull swimmers underwater. It is also called a *rip current*. This is a strong channel of water. It can drag people away from the beach. They may fight to stay above the surface. Even strong swimmers struggle. Surfers or swimmers should swim parallel to the beach to get out of a rip current. This is very important to know!

1. Which question about the text would help readers monitor their reading?
   - (A) How do you get sand out of your shoes?
   - (B) How did I get this rip in my pants?
   - (C) Why can swimming in the ocean be dangerous?
   - (D) What do kids learn in swimming lessons?

2. Which new title best fits the text?
   - (A) "Beach Fun"
   - (B) "Safety in the Water"
   - (C) "Playing with Beach Balls"
   - (D) "Swimming in the Pool"

3. What is the definition of *drag* as it is used in this text?
   - (A) moving slowly
   - (B) a nuisance
   - (C) pulling someone
   - (D) effort

4. Which word describes the tone of this text?
   - (A) warning
   - (B) sad
   - (C) funny
   - (D) historical

5. According to the text, what should you do if you are ever caught in a riptide?
   - (A) call out for help
   - (B) swim back to shore
   - (C) swim parallel to the beach
   - (D) hold your breath underwater until the tide calms down

Directions: Write two new words you can make using only the letters of each spelling word. An example has been done for you.

1. eight

   tie ______ get ______

2. fifth

   ______ ______

3. fourth

   ______ ______

4. hundred

   ______ ______

5. number

   ______ ______

6. second

   ______ ______

7. seventh

   ______ ______

8. sixth

   ______ ______

9. third

   ______ ______

10. twelve

   ______ ______

Directions: Answer each question.

1. Rewrite the sentence using an apostrophe.

   The friend of Jason was trying to organize a kickball game.

   ____

   ____

2. Rewrite the sentence using an apostrophe.

   The lunch box belonging to Ted was in the lost and found.

   ____

   ____

3. Write *the dog belonging to Rita* in another way.

   ____

4. Write *the baby brother of Hector* in another way.

   ____

5. Write *the birthday party of Desi* in another way.

   ____

6. Add apostrophes to the sentence.

   Rosies soccer uniform was mixed up with her sisters uniform.

Directions: Some animals are wild. Other animals are pets. What makes an animal a pet? Write the characteristics of pets in the outer bubbles.

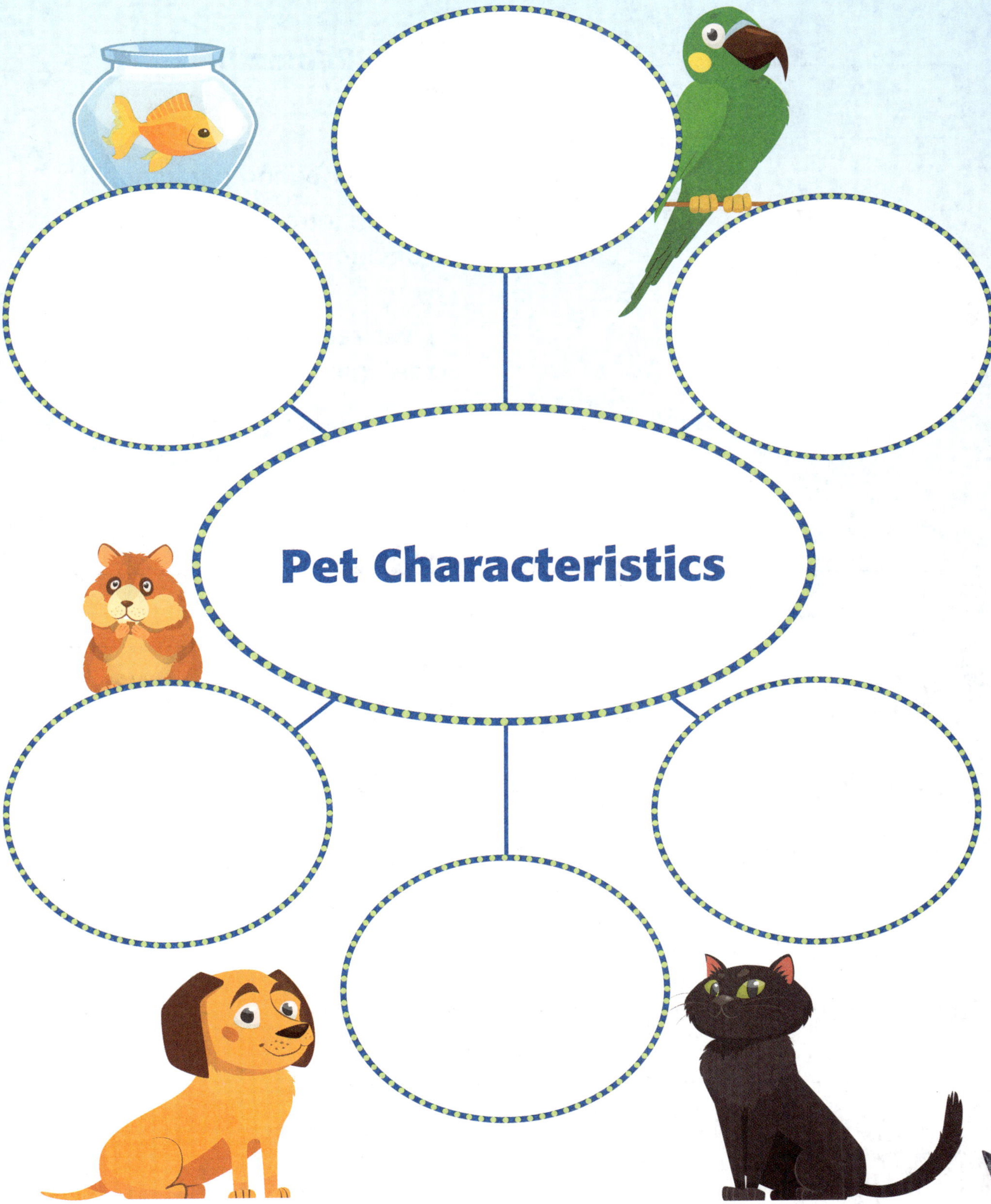

Directions: Write an opinion paragraph about which animal you think makes the best pet. Be sure to include reasons to support your opinion. Use the notes from page 71 to help you.

Remember!

A strong opinion paragraph:

- has an introductory and a concluding sentence stating your opinion
- gives reasons that support the opinion

Directions: Solve each problem.

1. Round 125 to the nearest ten.

   ____

2. Round 175 to the nearest hundred.

   ____

3. Round 64 to the nearest ten.

   ____

4. Round 834 to the nearest hundred.

   ____

5. Round 743 to the nearest ten.

   ____

6. Round 743 to the nearest hundred.

   ____

7. Round 351 to the nearest ten.

   ____

8. Round 351 to the nearest hundred.

   ____

Directions: Solve each problem.

1. Record the area.

_____________ square units

2. Circle the solid that has a greater volume.

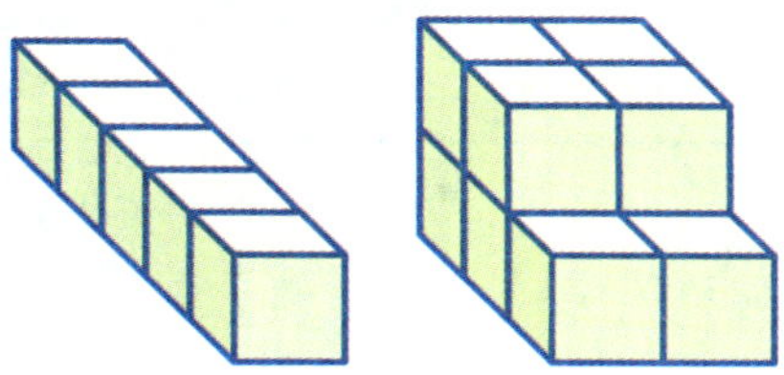

3. Record the area.

_____________ square units

4. Circle the solid that has less volume.

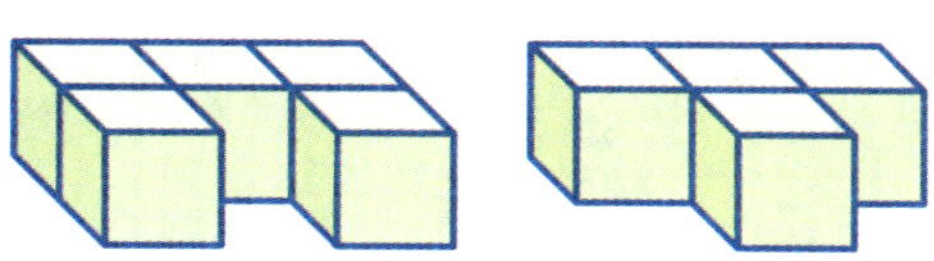

5. Circle the solid that has a greater volume.

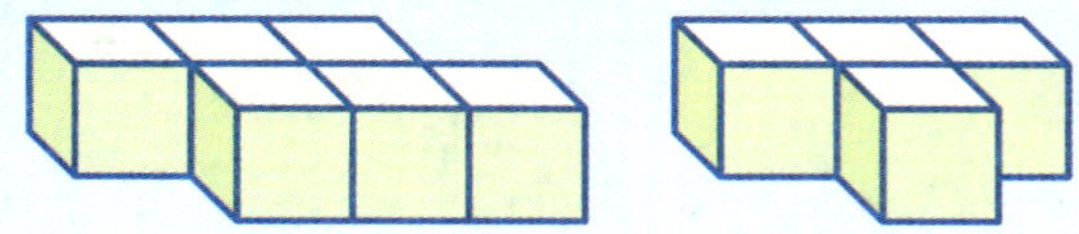

6. Record the area.

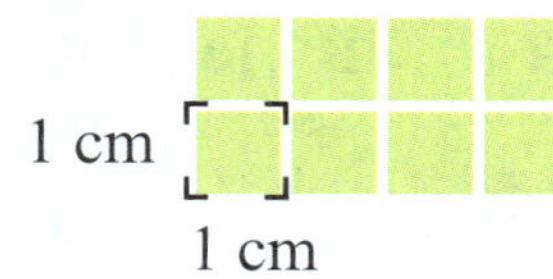

_____________ cm^2

7. How many cubic centimeters are in the solid?

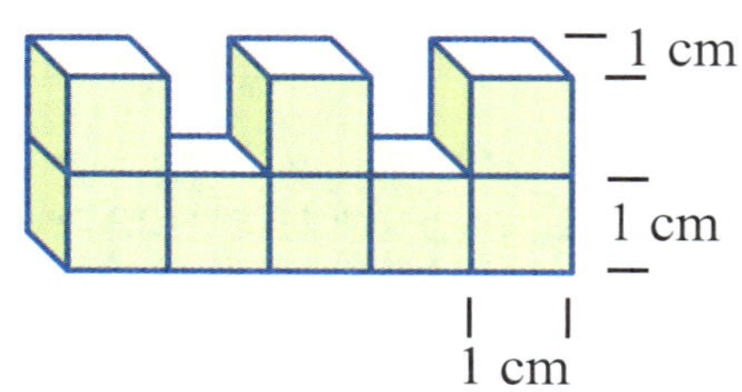

_____________ cm^3

8. What is the volume of the solid?

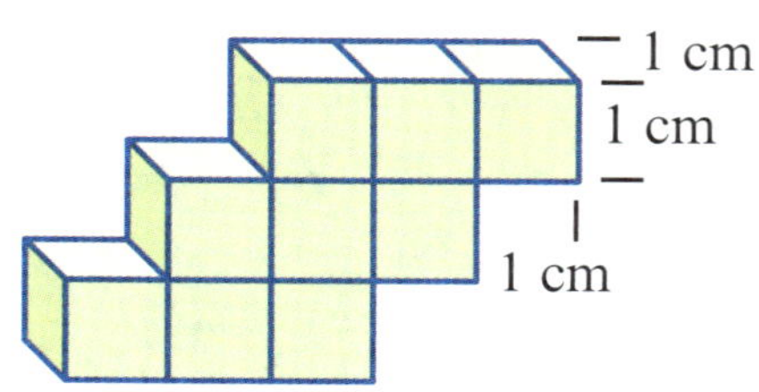

_____________ cm^3

Directions: Look at the example. Then, solve the problem.

Example: Break apart the first factor into two addends. Use them as factors to find the product.

7 × 8 = ☐

5 + 2

5 × 8 = 40
2 × 8 = 16
40 + 16 = 56

1. Break apart the first factor into two addends. Use them as factors to find the product.

8 × 6 = ☐

5 + ____

5 × ____ = ____
____ × ____ = ____
____ + ____ = ____

2. Break apart the first factor into two addends. Use them as factors to find the product.

6 × 9 = ☐

3 + ____

3 × ____ = ____
____ × ____ = ____
____ + ____ = ____

Directions: Show two ways to solve the problem.

1. Antonio is running for class president. He made flyers for his campaign. Eight of his friends will help hand them out. Each friend has 9 flyers. How many flyers will they hand out?

Strategy 1

Strategy 2

2. Which strategy do you prefer? Explain your reasoning.

____

____

____

Directions: Read the historical background. Then, read the First Amendment in the Bill of Rights, and answer the questions.

Historical Background

The United States Constitution is the highest set of laws in the United States. It tells American leaders and citizens how the country should be run. In 1791, the Bill of Rights was added to the U.S. Constitution. This is a set of 10 amendments, or changes, to the Constitution. It was written to protect the rights of American citizens.

Amendment I

Congress shall make no law respecting an establishment of religion, or prohibiting the free exercise thereof; or abridging the freedom of speech, or of the press; or the right of the people peaceably to assemble, and to petition the government for a redress of grievances.

1. Look up words you don't know, and think about their meanings.

2. What rights does the First Amendment give citizens? Hint: Look for the words *freedom*, *free*, and *right*.

____

____

____

____

____

Directions: Follow the steps in this experiment to discover how many bones are in your hands.

What You Need

colored pencils

What to Do

1. Look at the diagram of the hand bones.

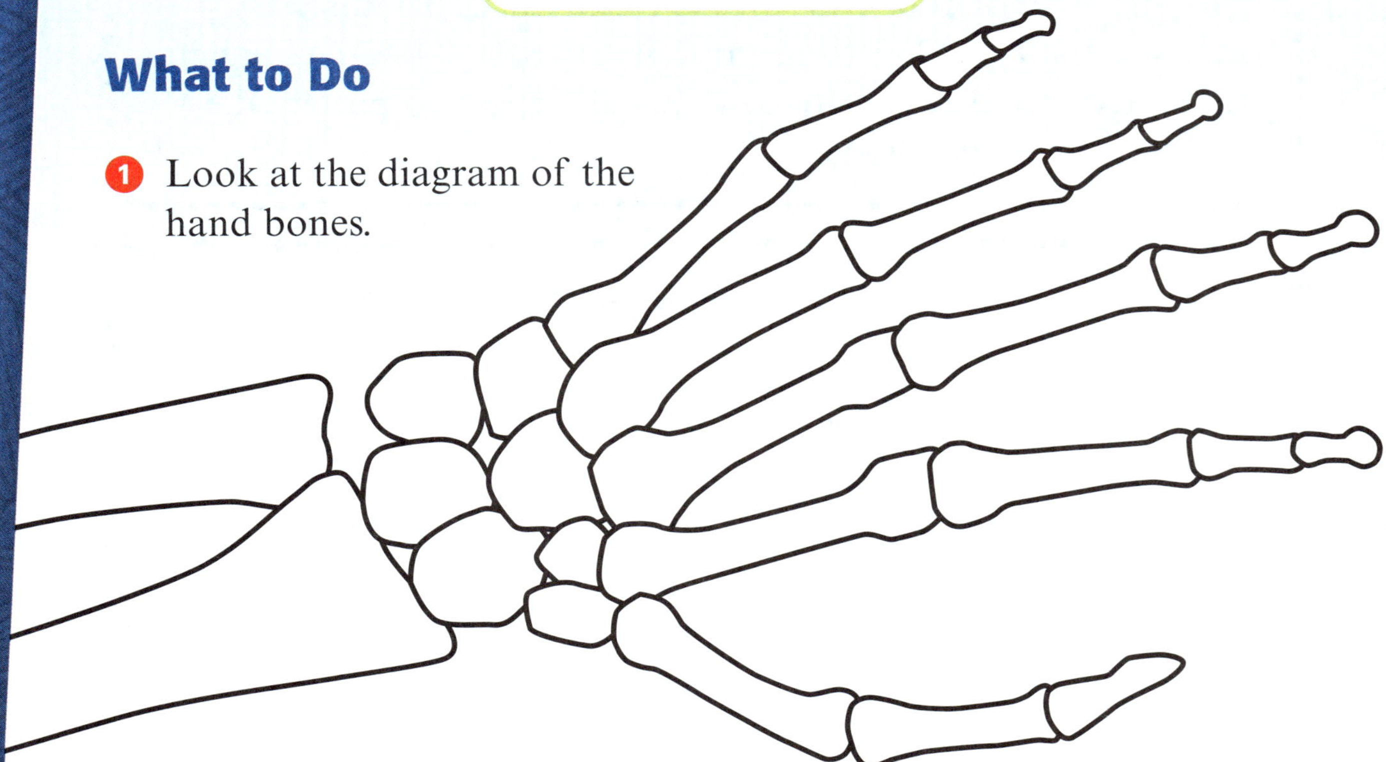

2. Feel your hand. Try to feel the bones shown in the diagram. How many bones can you find?

____

3. Use blue to color the bones in the diagram that you can feel.
4. Use red to color the bones in the diagram that you cannot feel.
5. Draw an outline of your hand around the diagram. Hint: Think about which bones are in your fingers and which are in your palm before you begin drawing.

Directions: Read the clues to label each person's house.

1 ____________________ 2 ____________________ 3 ____________________

4 ____________________ 5 ____________________ 6 ____________________

Clues

- Colin's house is on one end of the street. It has two stories and a chimney.
- Meg's house has two stories. It does not have a garage.
- Ralph's house is red and has only one story.
- Lin's house has a front porch, but it does not have a chimney.
- Tara's house is to the right of Colin's.
- Tyrone's house is white and has a chimney.

Directions: Work with a partner. Take turns rolling three number cubes 10 times. Write a three-digit number using the numbers you rolled. Then, round that number to the nearest ten and the nearest hundred.

Example:

Number	Nearest Ten	Nearest Hundred
146	150	100

Number	Nearest Ten	Nearest Hundred

Spelling Activity

Choose two of the words on page 69. Use the letters from both words to write as many new words as possible.

Problem-Solving Activity

Take turns rolling two number cubes with a partner. Multiply the two numbers. Use different strategies to prove that your answers are correct.

Social Studies Activity

Have an adult help you read other amendments from the Bill of Rights aloud. Talk about what rights are protected by these amendments and how they affect Americans today.

Science Activity

Find a diagram of the bones in the foot. See how many bones you can feel in your foot.

Writing Activity

Write a funny story about a wild animal that someone tried to adopt as a pet.

Critical-Thinking Activity

Draw pictures of five toys. Then, write clues about each toy. Ask someone to use your clues to figure out who owns each toy.

Directions: Read the text, and answer the questions on the next page.

A Different Kind of Princess

Once upon a time, a princess lived in a castle. She lived with her mother and father, the king and queen. She had no brothers or sisters. As she grew up, her parents began to talk to her about whom she might marry. Her marriage would be very important. Her husband would inherit the throne.

Many princesses wait for the day they can marry a handsome prince. Yet this was no ordinary princess. She preferred her hunting clothes to any elegant dress. She wore her hair in a ponytail instead of having long waves topped with a tiara. She hated spending her days in the castle. She did not like to just sit around and do nothing. The princess always tried to find someone to take her out to the forest. She would ride a horse and feel the wind blow through her hair. She loved adventure.

On this day, the princess did not want to talk about a marriage. She was not going to marry anyone that her parents had selected for her. She wasn't even sure she wanted to be married at all. Today, she just wanted to ride her horse.

She walked around the castle. Finally, she found a servant boy. She asked him to help her get a horse ready to ride. They talked a lot, and the princess enjoyed his company. The servant boy was surprised by the princess. He expected her to be snobby, but he liked talking to her, too. The princess wondered why she could not spend more time with boys like him. Why did her parents only introduce her to the sons of their friends? All this princess knew was that things were going to change. She was going to spend some time with her new friend. She was going to make her own decisions. She was going to be a different kind of princess.

Directions: Read "A Different Kind of Princess," and then answer the questions.

1. Which is most likely the author's opinion?
   - Ⓐ A story set in a castle must have a happy ending.
   - Ⓑ A princess with no magic is sad.
   - Ⓒ Princesses can look, sound, and think differently.
   - Ⓓ All princesses want to find a handsome prince.

2. Which statement shows a personal connection to this text?
   - Ⓐ I don't like to do things that most girls do.
   - Ⓑ I saw a castle in a movie.
   - Ⓒ I have four sisters.
   - Ⓓ I read a book about a family that has servants.

3. Which quality of the princess makes her a different kind of princess?
   - Ⓐ She does not like wearing a tiara.
   - Ⓑ She does not want to get married to a prince right away.
   - Ⓒ She likes to talk to servants.
   - Ⓓ all of the above

4. Why is this fairy tale different from many other fairy tales?
   - Ⓐ Most fairy tales do not include horseback riding.
   - Ⓑ Most fairy tales include a princess who is looking for a prince.
   - Ⓒ Most fairy tales include wicked stepsisters.
   - Ⓓ Most fairy tales do not include servants.

Directions: Unscramble each word. Use the Word Bank to help you.

Word Bank

- almost
- children
- follow
- largest
- heard
- picture
- spelling
- beside
- either
- wrong

Scrambled Word	Unscrambled Word
1 lpiesnlg	
2 ergtsla	
3 cuptier	
4 ogwrn	
5 nhrdceli	
6 hraed	
7 mtloas	
8 reethi	
9 loolfw	
10 sedebi	

Directions: Answer each question.

1. Circle the adverbs in the sentence.

   Kara lovingly hugged her sister before she quickly boarded the plane.

2. Circle the adverbs in the sentence.

   Good friends almost always play happily together.

3. Circle the adverbs in the sentence.

   The rain fell quietly while I slept peacefully in my bed.

4. Circle the adverbs in the sentence.

   The bicycle zoomed by quickly as it sped down the hill.

5. Write two adverbs that could be used in the sentence.

   Our family's pet cat always naps ________________ and ________________ in the sun.

6. Write a sentence using an adverb. Circle the adverb.

   ____

   ____

Directions: Name four different types of land transportation. Then, write a sentence about each of them. Hint: Think about things that can move goods, a single person, or a group of people.

1. ____________________ : ____

____

____

2. ____________________ : ____

____

____

3. ____________________ : ____

____

____

4. ____________________ : ____

____

____

Directions: Imagine traveling somewhere by land. Write a narrative paragraph describing your experience. Be sure to include characters, setting, problem(s), rising action, and a solution. Use your notes from page 86 to help you.

Edit and Revise!

Be sure that you check your writing for:

- an introductory and concluding sentence
- sensory details to describe the experience
- correct spelling, punctuation, and capitalization

Directions: Solve each problem.

1. Nicole gets $12.00 in allowance each week. Every week, she saves $4.00 of it and spends the rest. How much does she spend in 4 weeks?

   ____

2. Collin has to read a book that has 63 pages in it. He has to have it read in one week. How many pages should he read each day to be done in time?

   ____

3. A monkey eats 6 bananas a day. How many bananas will it eat in 2 weeks?

   ____

4. Jack walks his dog for 20 minutes each morning and 10 minutes each night. How many minutes does he walk his dog in 3 days?

   ____

5. A teddy bear costs $12.50. Jack has $26.00. He wants to buy two teddy bears. Does Jack have enough money?

   ____

6. Isabel can make a bow with 12 inches of ribbon. There are 4 yards of ribbon on a spool. How many bows can Isabel make with one spool of ribbon?

   ____

Directions: Solve each problem.

1. $\begin{array}{r} 12 \\ \times \ \ 8 \\ \hline \square \end{array}$

2. $\square \times 8 = 32$

3. $25 \div 5 = \square$

4. $\begin{array}{r} 7 \\ \times \ \ 6 \\ \hline \square \end{array}$

5. $\begin{array}{r} 10 \\ \times \ \ 6 \\ \hline \square \end{array}$

6. $24 \bigcirc 6 = 4$

7. $16 \div 4 = \square$

8. $9 \times \square = 27$

Directions: Read and solve the problem.

Stacy has 10 boxes of markers. Five of the boxes have 20 markers each. The other 5 boxes have 30 markers each. How many markers does she have in all?

1. Draw a model to show your work.

2. What is the solution? Explain how you found your answer.

Directions: Read and solve the problem.

Kim and Kevin are practicing their multiplication and division facts. Kim tells Kevin to find all the fact families he knows with the product 24. Kevin writes 4 fact families. What fact families did Kevin write?

1. Write the fact families with the product 24.

	×		=				×		=	
	×		=				×		=	
	÷		=				÷		=	
	÷		=				÷		=	
	×		=				×		=	
	×		=				×		=	
	÷		=				÷		=	
	÷		=				÷		=	

2. Choose one fact family you wrote. Draw a picture to show the fact family.

Directions: Look up a map of your city online or using a navigation app. Draw a map of your city. Use symbols to show your home, your school, and other important places. Label your symbols in the legend.

Legend

Directions: Follow the steps in this experiment to see which items are conductors. Have an adult help you.

What You Need

- hammer
- C battery
- electrical wire
- two steel nails
- light bulb
- small objects
- block of wood or Styrofoam
- metal paper clip

What to Do

1. Hammer the two nails into the block, 2 cm apart.
2. Use electrical wire to attach the battery to one nail. Attach the light bulb to the other nail. Then, use a third piece of wire to connect the light bulb to the other end of the battery.
3. Place a paper clip across the nails on the block. The light should turn on. The paper clip is a conductor.
4. Now, test to see if any of the small objects are also conductors. Place each one across the nails on the block. Record your results.

Item	Conductor?
metal paper clip	

Directions: Kay and Josh created a secret code using symbols and numbers. Use the key to decode their message. Then, write your own message.

Key

A	B	C	D	E	F	G	H	I
!	@	#	$	%	^	&	*	+
J	K	L	M	N	O	P	Q	R
?	>	<	=	{	}	\	1	2
S	T	U	V	W	X	Y	Z	
3	4	5	6	7	8	9	10	

Kay and Josh's Message

___ ___ ___ ___   ___ ___   ___ ___

 # } = %   4 }   = 9

___ ___ ___ ___ ___   ___ ___   ___ ___ ___ ___

*** } 5 3 %   4 }   \ < ! 9**

Your Message

____

____

____

____

Directions: Play with a partner. Each player should place a small object at the start. Take turns rolling a number cube. Move your object to number of spaces that you roll. Solve the problem in the space where you land. The first player to reach the finish line wins.

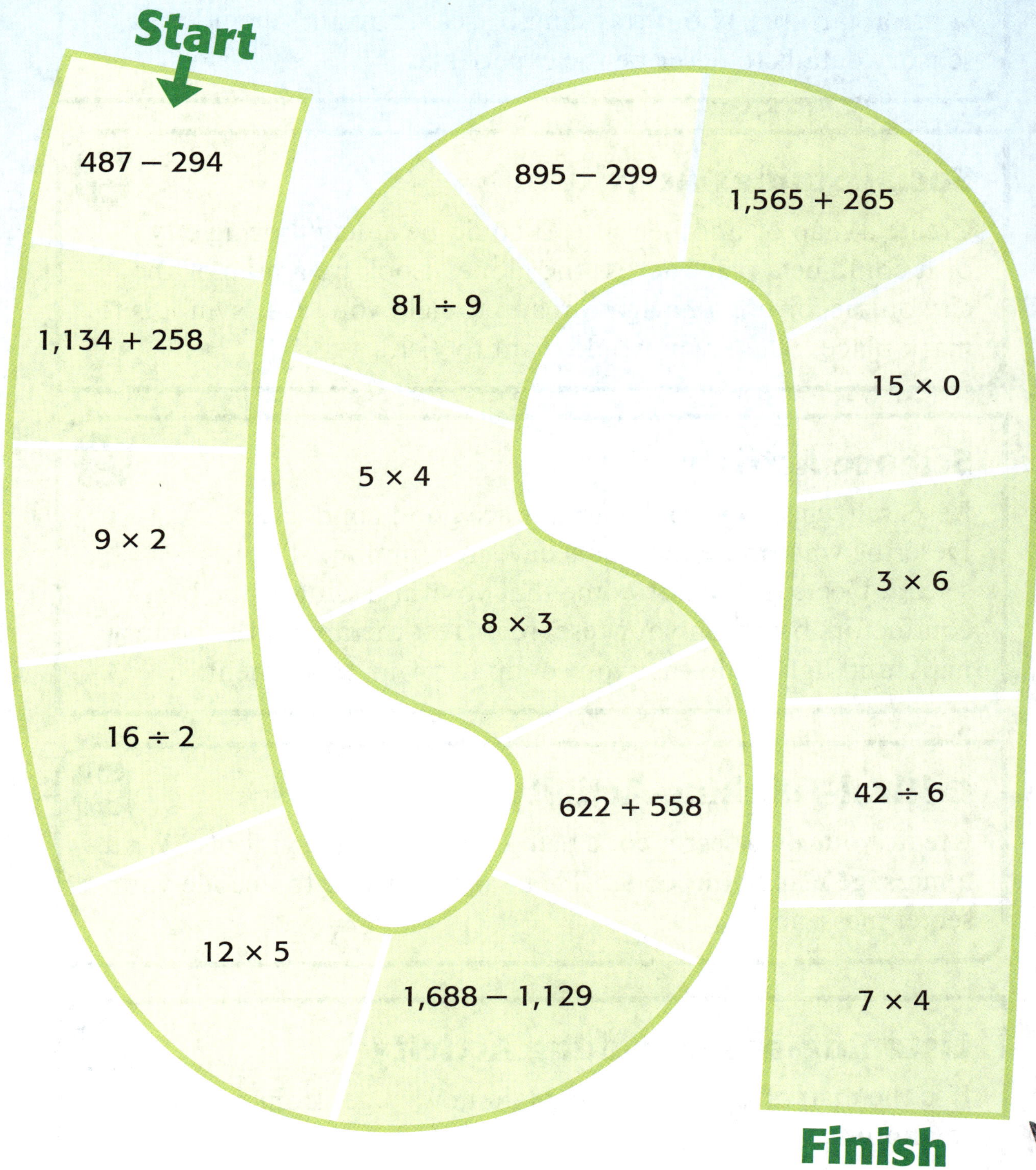

Spelling Activity

Challenge yourself to write a funny story using all the spelling words on page 84. Use your best cursive handwriting.

Writing Activity

Write a narrative about traveling by sea or by air. Include sensory details to describe the experience.

Social Studies Activity

Create a map of another city. It could be a neighboring city, or it could be a place across the globe. Look up a map of the city online, or use a navigation app to help you. Use symbols to mark places where you would want to visit.

Science Activity

Research what types of materials are good conductors. Describe what these materials have in common. Then, select objects from your home that you think will be the best conductors based on your research. Test them with the battery, nails, and light bulb that you set up for your experiment.

Critical-Thinking Activity

Create your own secret code using numbers and symbols. Write a message using your code. Then, ask someone to decode your secret message.

Listening-and-Speaking Activity

Use the map of your city to explain how to get from one place to another.

Directions: Read the text, and answer the questions on the next page.

Julius Caesar

Julius Caesar is an important person in history. He was an ancient Roman leader. Caesar was born in 100 BC. He grew up in a simple home. His family belonged to an old Roman family. They were neither rich nor poor.

Most boys like Caesar did not go to school. They had tutors instead. Caesar learned a lot from his tutor. He learned to read and write Latin. He also became a good public speaker. These skills would help him later in life.

Caesar fell in love with a girl named Cornelia. They married and had a daughter. They all lived together in Rome. Caesar rose to power as time went on. He was given important jobs, and people started to see him as a leader.

Caesar had joined the Roman army at a young age. He quickly became a leader. The troops liked him, and people respected him. He won many battles for Rome. The Roman army was very powerful. Having the respect of that army was a very big deal.

Back in Rome, the leaders were in trouble. The republic was in shambles, and leaders were arguing. Finally, the Senate was forced to change. Three men took over as leaders. One of them was Julius Caesar. Soon after, Caesar was fighting for power. He took over as the only leader of Rome. He made himself a dictator. This made people upset. Romans did not want a king, and a dictator was too much like a king. They did not want Caesar to change their lives too much. Some members of the Senate decided to kill Caesar. He was stabbed to death. The day he was killed is known as the *ides of March*.

Many men ruled Rome after Caesar. Some were good leaders. Some were not. The Roman Empire changed over the years. Caesar will always be remembered as an important leader.

Directions: Read "Julius Caesar," and then answer the questions.

1. What is the purpose for reading this text?
   - (A) to read a biography of Julius Caesar
   - (B) to be entertained by facts about Roman life
   - (C) to learn about Roman army strategies
   - (D) to learn how to be a good leader

2. Which statement would the author likely agree with?
   - (A) Caesar should have never gotten married.
   - (B) Caesar was a leader who tried to get too much power.
   - (C) Caesar was a better soldier than a leader.
   - (D) Caesar didn't know how to lead.

3. Whom did Caesar fight for power?
   - (A) Cornelia
   - (B) his tutor
   - (C) the Roman army
   - (D) two other leaders

4. How is this text organized?
   - (A) as a comparison of Julius Caesar and Cornelia
   - (B) as a chronological history of Julius Caesar's life
   - (C) as a list of steps for how to join the army
   - (D) as a chronological history of Roman battles

5. What alternative title reflects the main idea of the text?
   - (A) "Leader of the Army"
   - (B) "The Success and Struggles of Julius Caesar"
   - (C) "A Smart Marriage"
   - (D) "Betrayed by the Man"

6. What mistake led to Caesar's death?
   - (A) He did not know how to lead.
   - (B) He was not smart enough.
   - (C) The army did not respect him.
   - (D) He tried to have too much power.

Directions: Write each word. Then, write each word backward.

1. aunt ____________ ____________
2. brother ____________ ____________
3. daughter ____________ ____________
4. father ____________ ____________
5. grandfather ____________ ____________
6. grandmother ____________ ____________
7. mother ____________ ____________
8. sister ____________ ____________
9. son ____________ ____________
10. uncle ____________ ____________

Directions: Answer each question.

1. Write a sentence using the word *education.*

2. Write a sentence using an adjective to describe an object in your bedroom.

3. Write a sentence using an adverb that describes how you moved in the morning.

4. Write a sentence using the word *determination.*

5. Write a sentence using the word *quest.*

Directions: Label the picture of the shark with the phrases from the Fact Bank.

Fact Bank

- skinny gills
- beady eye
- rough skin
- small fin
- sharp teeth
- pointy snout

Directions: Write an informative/explanatory paragraph about sharks. Include facts about what they eat and what they look like. Use your notes and the facts on page 101 to help you.

Edit and Revise!

Be sure that you check your writing for:

- a topic sentence
- details to support the main idea
- a concluding sentence

Directions: Solve each problem.

1. If each bottle holds 2 liters, what is the total capacity of all of the bottles?

____

2. How many full pitchers will it take to fill the bucket?

____

3. How many cups are there in a quart?

____

4. What is the total capacity of the mugs below?

____

5. Rocks were used to measure the mass of each object. Circle the object with the greatest mass.

1 rock | 15 rocks | 3 rocks

6. Is the mass of a nail more or less than one kilogram?

____

7. Cubes were used to measure the mass of each box. Circle the container with the greatest mass.

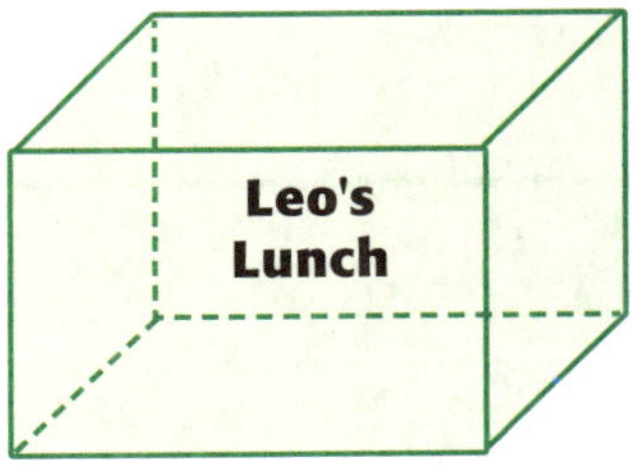

720 cubes

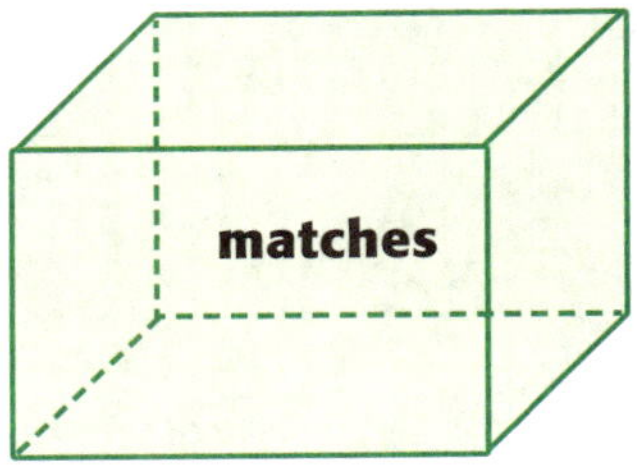

80 cubes

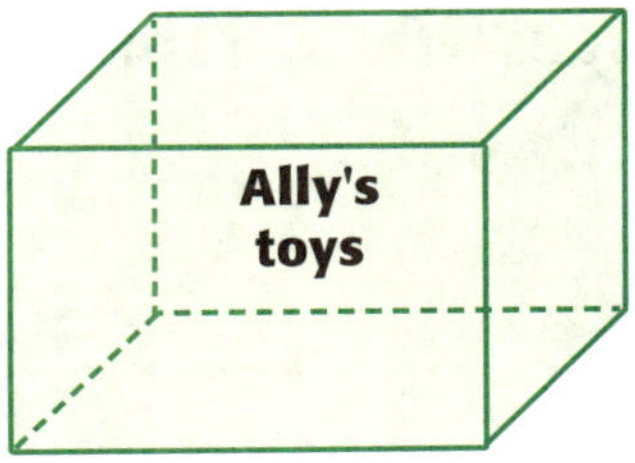

4,000 cubes

Directions: Solve each problem.

1. Fill in the bar graph based on the number of parts of the robot.

Parts of the Robot

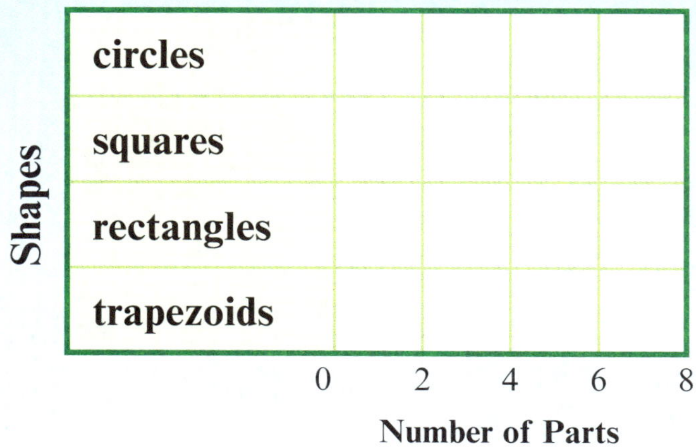

2. There are 6 oranges. There is one fewer apple than there are oranges. Complete the bar graph showing this data.

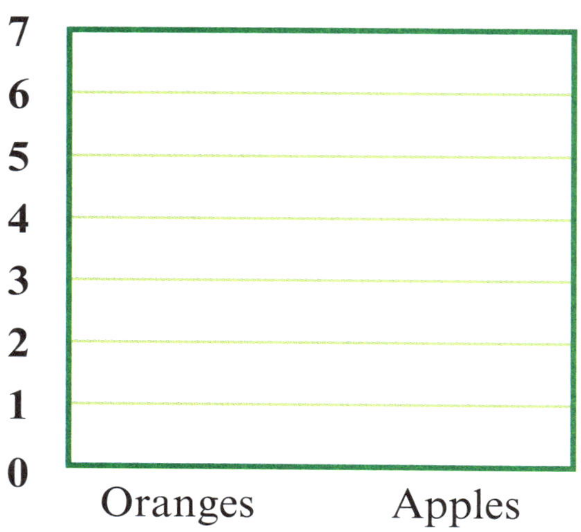

3. Study the chart. Answer the questions.

Favorite Subject in School

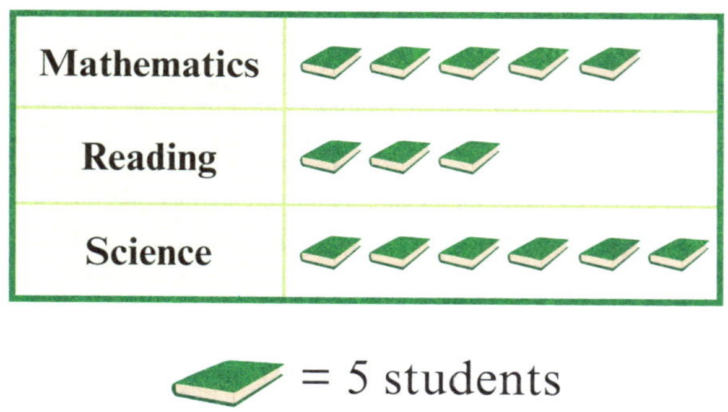

How many students prefer mathematics?

____

How many students prefer science than reading?

____

Directions: Read and solve the problem.

Dolly's Pie Shop sells pieces of pie. Each pie is cut into 6 pieces. Sam bought 6 pies. Nine people will share them. How many pieces of pie will each person get?

1. How many pieces of pie does Sam buy? Draw a picture to show your answer.

2. What is the solution? Explain your reasoning.

Directions: Read and solve the problem.

Julie wants to buy a new bike. The bike costs \$225. She gets an allowance of \$10 a week and has been saving for 7 weeks. She also earned \$112 for babysitting. Does Julie have enough money to buy the bike?

1. How much money does Julie have? Write equations to show the answer.

____

____

____

2. Solve the problem. Justify your answer.

____

____

____

Directions: Research another country and the people who live there. Use what you learn to complete the chart. Then, answer the questions.

Country: ______________________________

Weather	Neighboring Countries
Food	**Celebrations**

1. What did you find most interesting about this country? Why?

   ____

   ____

2. How is life in this country similar to and different from where you live?

   ____

   ____

   ____

Directions: Follow the steps in this experiment to discover how acidic water is in your local environment.

What You Need

- bucket
- 3 plastic jars
- rainwater
- tap water
- vinegar
- litmus paper

What to Do

1. On a stormy day, place the bucket outside in an open area. Let the bucket collect enough water to fill a jar partway. If rain is not likely for a while, collect water from a local lake, river, or the ocean to test instead.
2. Fill one jar with tap water, one with rainwater, and the other with vinegar. Label each jar.
3. Place a separate piece of litmus paper in each jar. Record what happens to the litmus paper. Note: The lower the number, the more acidic the liquid.

Tap Water	Rainwater	Vinegar

The most acidic liquid was: ______________________________

Directions: Read and follow the list of directions. Use each answer in the next problem. You should end with the same number you started with. Then, create your own list of directions that begins and ends with the same number.

1. Begin with the number 5.

   ____

2. Double it.

   ____

3. Add 15.

   ____

4. Multiply by 3.

   ____

5. Subtract 50.

   ____

6. Divide by 5.

   ____

Directions: Work with a partner. Use small objects to mark your spots on the game board. Take turns rolling a number cube. Move the number of spaces that you roll. Multiply the numbers in the space you land on. The first person to reach the finish line wins.

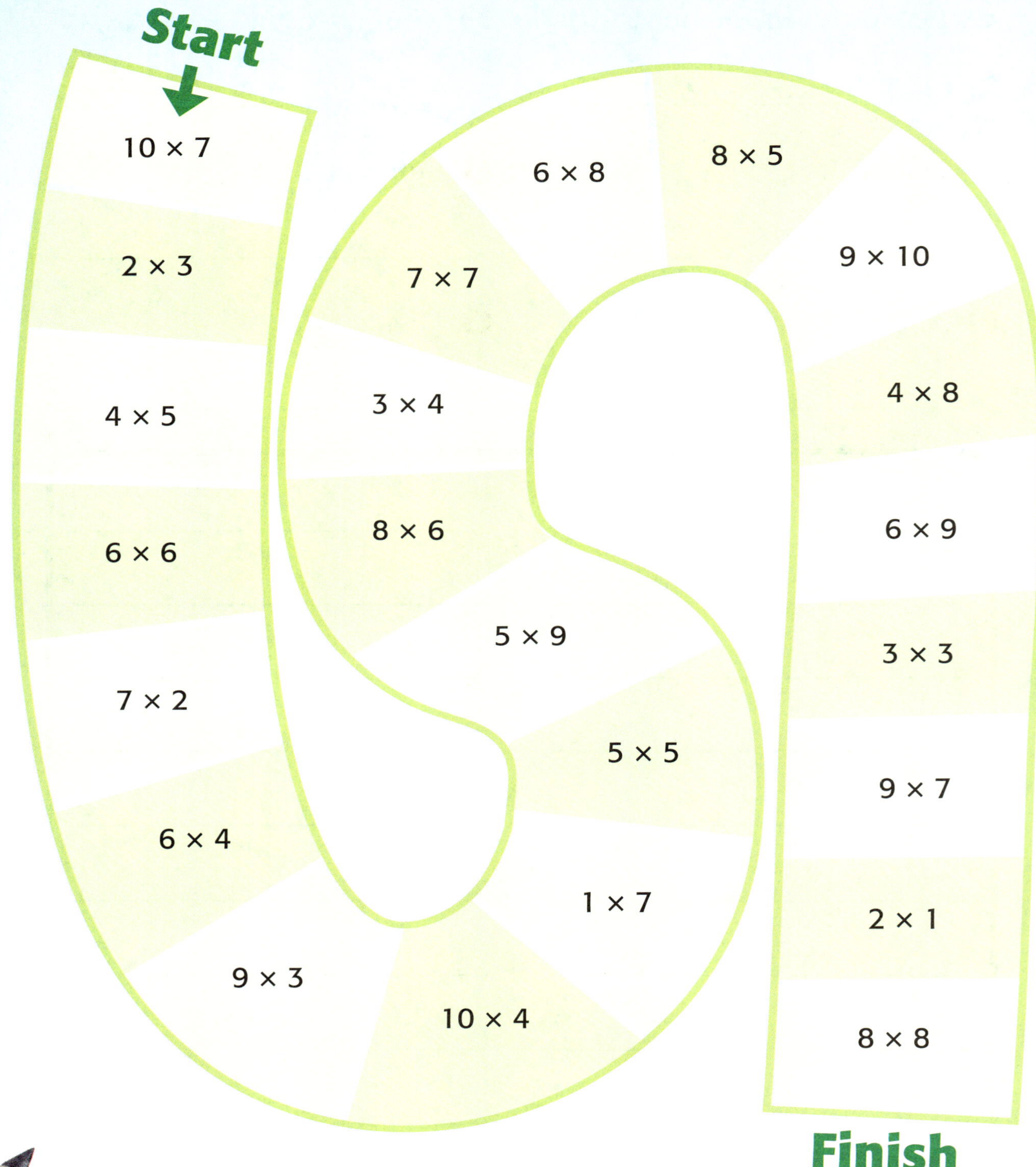

Spelling Activity

Draw a picture of your family. Use the spelling words on page 99 to label your family picture.

Mathematics Activity

At the market or around your home, look for liquid measurements on water bottles, juice boxes, or other containers. Compare the measurements of various containers. In what units are the measurements listed? What are some common sizes for liquid containers?

Science Activity

Test the acidity of other liquids in your daily life. You could test juice, milk, chicken soup, and water in swimming pools. What else could you test? Which liquid is the most acidic?

Social Studies Activity

Share what you learned about another country with your family. Explain what you found most interesting and why. Then, research more about the country's culture together.

Listening-and-Speaking Activity

Ask a family member if they have ever been to another country. If so, ask him or her to describe it to you. Ask questions to learn more about the country and its people. If this family member has not been to another country, ask which country he or she would most like to visit and why.

Directions: Read the text, and answer the questions on the next page.

A Magical Discovery Time

From a young age, Chester knew he was different. He had a feeling inside that he had special powers. Chester knew this, yet he decided to keep it a secret. He was not sure how his family would feel or whether his friends would understand. Kids don't always want to feel different from others, and Chester was no exception.

The first clue came when he was four years old. He was playing in his sandbox in the backyard when he saw a beautiful butterfly. He put it on his hand. Then, he realized the butterfly was dead. Chester felt so sad about the butterfly that he began to cry, and tears started to fall down his face. A tear landed on the butterfly, and it instantly came to life! Chester could not believe his eyes.

It took Chester several more years to figure out what made him special. By the time he was eight, he knew all of his powers. He could bring things back to life, he could fly, he could see through walls, and he could hear things from a great distance. These skills excited him, yet he also felt very alone. No one else could know about these incredible powers. He didn't know anyone else who had them.

One day, he walked into his third grade classroom. Chester was early, and he was the first student there. Then, Fiona walked in, seeming to appear out of nowhere. When she came in the room, she stopped and looked at the classroom wall. "I guess Room 215 has a substitute teacher today," she said.

Chester stopped in his tracks. How did she know that? Room 215 was next door. Could Fiona see through the wall? He was puzzled. Then, he saw the smile on Fiona's face as she stared at him. He knew he had found a partner in magic.

Directions: Read "A Magical Discovery Time," and then answer the questions.

1. Which prediction makes sense after reading the title?
   - (A) This story must have a happy ending.
   - (B) This story includes magic.
   - (C) This story happens during a single day.
   - (D) This story takes place at the circus.

2. What is the author's purpose?
   - (A) to compare Chester and Fiona's magical powers
   - (B) to engage readers and have them use their imaginations
   - (C) to teach readers how to use magic
   - (D) to explain about substitute teachers

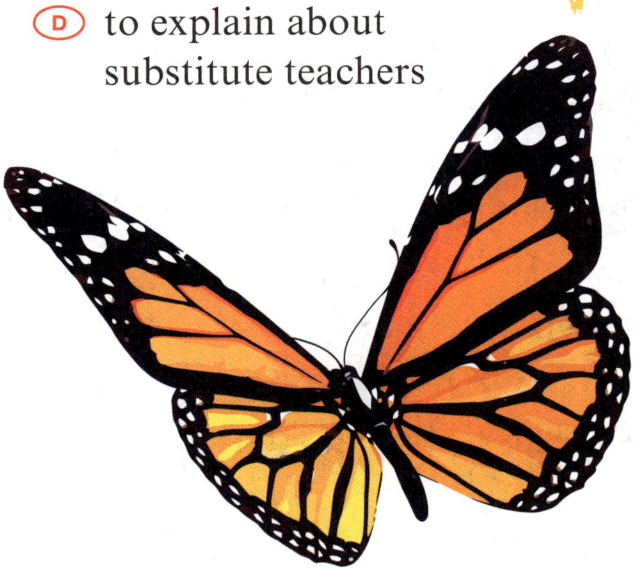

3. How does Chester feel about his magical powers?
   - (A) He feels lucky.
   - (B) He feels excited yet alone.
   - (C) He feels frightened.
   - (D) He feels special.

4. Which theme applies to this text?
   - (A) Keeping secrets can keep you safe.
   - (B) Substitute teachers are horrible.
   - (C) Grown-ups do not understand kids.
   - (D) Having a friend makes life less lonely.

5. What other type of text is similar to this one?
   - (A) a fantasy about aliens
   - (B) a how-to book on magic
   - (C) a realistic fictional story about feeling different
   - (D) a nonfiction adventure about a scientific discovery

UNIT 8

Spelling

Directions: Complete the sentences with words from the Word Bank.

Word Bank

- already
- below
- desert
- forgot
- might
- nothing
- sorry
- study
- tonight
- which

1. I ________________ my lunch at home, so my mom brought it to school.

2. Kevin was ________________ that he accidentally bumped into Margot.

3. Tim ________________ has a toy car, so he gave Matt his extra one.

4. Ray found his story on the bulletin board ________________ Misha's story.

5. The ________________ is a hot, dry, and sandy place in the summer.

6. Mom said she ________________ buy me a new bike for my birthday.

7. Be sure to ________________ for the test tomorrow.

8. ________________ shirt do you think I should wear for picture day?

9. Dad asked me where I want to go for dinner ________________ .

10. Preston searched his pockets for his lost money, but he found ________________ .

Directions: Answer each question.

1. Circle the words in the sentence that need capital letters.

   It is difficult to play the song "stomping along" on the piano.

2. Circle the words in the sentence that need capital letters.

   How many syllables are in the haiku poem titled "the beautiful forest"?

3. Circle the words that need capital letters.

   "Hey, Mom, I just noticed that the video game titled *baseball championship* is on sale," said Rodrigo.

4. Circle the types of words that are always capitalized.

   song titles　　compound words　　adjectives

5. Circle the words that need capital letters.

   I think I know all of the words to the song "uncle john's farm."

6. Circle the types of words that are always capitalized.

   long words　　titles of poems　　the last words in sentences

Directions: Read the statement. Then, write at least five reasons in each column.

Ice cream is the best dessert.

Agree	Disagree

Directions: Do you think ice cream is the best dessert? Write an opinion paragraph explaining your thoughts. Give at least three reasons to support your opinion. Use your notes from page 116 to help you.

Edit and Revise!

Be sure that you check your writing for:

- introductory and concluding sentences
- details that support your opinion

Directions: Solve each problem.

1. How many are in 7 groups of 9?

____

2. Draw 5 groups of 7 hats. How many hats are there?

____

3. How many ears are there on 8 people?

____

4. Draw a 7 by 8 array.

5. Draw an array with 6 rows of 1.

6. How many are in 4 groups of 10?

____

Directions: Solve each problem.

1. Partition the square into four equal parts. Write a fraction for each part.

____

2. Partition the circle into two equal parts. Write a fraction for each part.

____

3. Partition the rectangle into three equal parts. Shade two of the parts, and write a fraction for the shaded part.

____

4. What fraction of the rectangle is shaded?

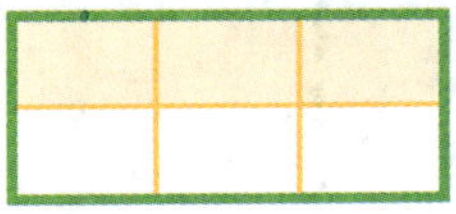

____

5. What fraction of the circle is shaded?

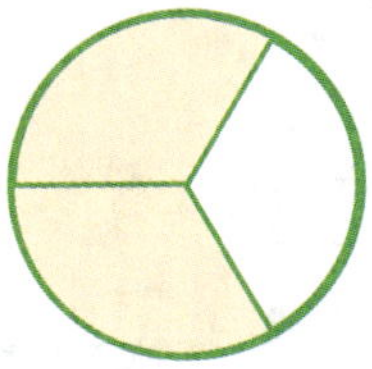

____

6. What fraction of the triangle is shaded?

____

7. Partition the circle four equal parts. Shade as many equal parts as you want. Write a fraction for the part you shaded.

____

Directions: Read and solve the problem.

Destiny and her dad bake a cake. Her dad cuts the cake into 6 equal pieces. Her family eats 3 pieces. She says, "We ate $\frac{1}{2}$ of the cake." Is Destiny correct?

1. Draw a model to show the problem.

2. Do you agree with Destiny? Why or why not?

Directions: Label the number line. Answer the questions. Then, draw and label a number line at the bottom of the page. Chose five fractions to label on your number line.

Draw a point and label each fraction on the number line.

$\frac{1}{2}$ $\frac{1}{3}$ $\frac{1}{4}$

0 1

1. Which fraction is closest to 0? ________
2. Which fraction is exactly in the middle of 0 and 1? ________
3. Explain your strategy for labeling the fractions.

____

____

____

____

Directions: Answer the questions. Then, choose a leader in your school, city, state, or country. Write about the qualities he or she has that make this person a good leader.

1. List the qualities that you think a good leader should have.

____

____

____

2. Which quality do you think is most important? Why?

____

____

____

Leader: ______________________________

____

____

____

____

____

____

____

Directions: Follow the steps in this experiment to discover how far things roll.

What You Need

- several books
- a wide piece of wood
- objects to roll
- yardstick

What to Do

1. Stack several books on a flat surface. Lay one end of the wood on the books and the other on the flat surface to create a ramp.
2. Roll different things down the ramp to see how far they go. Don't push them—just let them go.
3. Use the yardstick to measure how far each thing rolls. Record your results in the chart below.

Object	Distance

4. Which object rolled the shortest distance?

____

5. Which object rolled the longest distance?

____

Directions: Look at each set of words or numbers. Sort the words or numbers into two categories. Label the categories on each chart. Then, explain how you sorted them.

Set 1

lime	carrot	watermelon	kiwi
apple	pineapple	pea	banana
pear	green bean	strawberry	green pepper

Category:	**Category:**

How did you sort the set?

____

Set 2

3	13	67	28	567	73
100	42	120	235	54	36

Category:	**Category:**

How did you sort the set?

____

UNIT 8

Game

Directions: Take turns rolling two number cubes with a partner. After each roll, multiply the numbers on the cubes. Match the product to the word in the chart, and add a tally mark next to it. Read the word in a silly voice. Keep rolling until you have each rolled 20 times.

1	already		**12**	study	
2	below		**15**	tonight	
3	desert		**16**	which	
4	forgot		**18**	picture	
5	might		**20**	children	
6	nothing		**24**	weather	
8	yesterday		**25**	teacher	
9	tomorrow		**30**	depend	
10	sorry		**36**	afternoon	

1. Which word(s) did you roll the most?

____

2. Which word(s) did you roll the least?

____

Spelling Activity

List the spelling words on page 114 in alphabetical order and reverse alphabetical order. Use your best cursive handwriting.

Writing Activity

Write an opinion paragraph about the worst food you have ever eaten. Use strong reasons to support your opinion.

Mathematics Activity

After meals, estimate what fraction of the food is left in serving dishes. Explain your reasoning to your family members, and ask them if they agree with your estimate.

Science Activity

Revisit the experiment on page 123. Try to figure out what affects how far objects roll down the ramp. What changes can you make to the objects, to the ramp, or to the flat surface to get the longest roll?

Critical-Thinking Activity

Sort the sets of words and numbers on page 124 in as many ways as you can. Explain your reasoning each time.

Listening-and-Speaking Activity

With your family, discuss leaders they respect. Ask questions about what makes each of these people a good leader.

Directions: Read the text, and answer the questions on the next page.

Navigating with Maps

A map is a detailed image of an area. Maps show us where things are, and they also show us how to get somewhere. They show places that are large and small. There are maps of buildings and parks. There are maps of the entire world. All maps show a large area as a small drawing.

Maps are much smaller than the areas they represent. Maps have scales that show how the distance on a map relates to the real distance. Some maps have scales written as a ratio. It shows how one length compares to another length. An inch on a map might equal a certain number of feet or miles on land.

Maps include symbols for real things. The symbols depend on what the map is showing. For example, a large map of a state or a country may have symbols for cities, highways, and rivers. A smaller map of a town may have symbols for hospitals, schools, and libraries. These symbols are all listed in the *key*. The key shows each symbol and what it stands for on the map. Maps keep changing as streets, cities, and countries change.

People have been using maps for thousands of years. At one time, people used only paper maps. Today, people use a computerized type of map. It is called a *global positioning system,* or GPS. A GPS uses satellites that orbit Earth. They send signals to GPS receivers. They can show location, speed, and direction. Instead of a paper map, people use GPS receivers, which are often in phones and other devices. A map shows up on a screen. The map points people in the right direction by showing the route as they move along.

GPS receivers are also found on ships and airplanes. They help pilots and captains navigate as they travel. They show distance between locations. A GPS is used with many other instruments.

Directions: Read "Navigating with Maps," and then answer the questions.

1. What is the purpose for reading this text?
   - (A) to be entertained
   - (B) to be persuaded to buy a map
   - (C) to learn about maps
   - (D) to learn about direction

2. Which statement would the author likely agree with?
   - (A) Maps are only for people who need to go places.
   - (B) Maps are better than GPS receivers.
   - (C) Maps are not useful.
   - (D) Maps may look different but have the same purpose.

3. Which statement shows a prior experience related to the text?
   - (A) I don't think maps are helpful.
   - (B) I am curious about how keys unlock doors.
   - (C) I want to be a pilot when I grow up.
   - (D) I used a map to find my friend's house.

4. The fourth paragraph would work best in a _______ book.
   - (A) history
   - (B) art
   - (C) math
   - (D) how-to

5. What is the main idea?
   - (A) Maps are interesting, and they change over time.
   - (B) Maps do not always tell you what you need to know.
   - (C) Maps are made by pilots.
   - (D) A GPS receiver is not a map.

6. Why do maps change?
   - (A) because map companies want to make money
   - (B) because the world is changing
   - (C) so that people who make maps can keep their jobs
   - (D) because maps are usually wrong

Directions: Write two words you can make using the letters of each spelling word.

1. whistle ____________ ____________
2. question ____________ ____________
3. helpless ____________ ____________
4. forever ____________ ____________
5. around ____________ ____________
6. mistake ____________ ____________
7. between ____________ ____________
8. compare ____________ ____________
9. start ____________ ____________
10. scared ____________ ____________

Directions: Answer each question.

1. Add a comma to the following address.

   4430 Northwest 50th Street
   New York NY 89220

2. Add a comma to the following address.

   440 Hancock Way
   Oklahoma City OK 60550

3. Add a comma to the following address.

   3009 Hartford Road
   Chicago IL 75884

4. Add a comma to the following address.

   4009 Tellium Lane
   Jacksonville FL 89403

5. Find the address of somewhere you would like to visit. Write it on the lines. Be sure to include commas where needed.

   ____

   ____

   ____

Directions: Draw pictures of the sun and the moon. Write one thing that is similar between them and one thing that is different.

Sun	Moon

Similarity

____

____

____

Difference

____

____

____

Directions: Think about the sun and the moon. Write an informative/explanatory paragraph about the most interesting facts about them. Discuss their similarities and differences, too. Use your notes from page 131 to help you.

Edit and Revise!

Be sure that you check your writing for:

- a topic sentence
- details to support the main idea
- a concluding sentence

Directions: Write an equivalent fraction for each.

1. $\frac{3}{6} = \frac{\square}{2}$

2. $\frac{2}{3} = \frac{\square}{6}$

3. $\frac{4}{8} = \frac{\square}{\square}$

4. $\frac{4}{6} = \frac{\square}{\square}$

5. $\frac{2}{8} = \frac{\square}{4}$

6. $\frac{5}{10} = \frac{\square}{\square}$

7. $\frac{3}{9} = \frac{\square}{\square}$

8. $\frac{3}{8} = \frac{\square}{\square}$

9. $\frac{10}{12} = \frac{\square}{\square}$

10. $\frac{1}{2} = \frac{\square}{\square} = \frac{\square}{\square} = \frac{\square}{\square}$

Directions: Solve each problem. Use the first problem to help you solve the second one.

1. $9 \times 2 =$ ________ $90 \times 2 =$ ________

2. $4 \times 5 =$ ________ $40 \times 5 =$ ________

3. $3 \times 9 =$ ________ $3 \times 90 =$ ________

4. $1 \times 8 =$ ________ $10 \times 8 =$ ________

5. $5 \times 3 =$ ________ $50 \times 3 =$ ________

6. $7 \times 4 =$ ________ $7 \times 40 =$ ________

7. $2 \times 7 =$ ________ $20 \times 7 =$ ________

8. $9 \times 9 =$ ________ $90 \times 9 =$ ________

Directions: Read and solve the problem.

Joey and Max each have a small pizza. Joey ate $\frac{1}{2}$ of his pizza. Max ate $\frac{4}{8}$ of his pizza. Max thinks he ate more pizza than Joey. Is Max correct?

1. Draw a model to show the problem.

2. Do you agree with Max? Explain your reasoning.

3. What fraction of the pizza does Max have left over? How do you know?

Directions: Read and solve the problem.

Lori is making a bag of trail mix. She uses a recipe to make one serving. Compare the fractions. Then, write them in order from least to greatest.

Trail Mix Recipe

$\frac{3}{4}$ cup of peanuts $\frac{1}{3}$ cup of chocolate candies $\frac{1}{2}$ cup of raisins

1. Draw a model to show your answer.

2. Explain how you ordered the fractions from least to greatest.

____

____

____

Directions: Imagine a world without rules. At first, you might think it sounds fun. But, think about the consequences of a world without rules. Think about what they would look like in your home, school, city, and country. Draw a picture and write a sentence to show the consequences of no rules in each of these places.

Home	Community
____________________ ____________________	____________________ ____________________

City	Country
____________________ ____________________	____________________ ____________________

Directions: Follow the steps in this experiment to discover what is magnetic.

What You Need

- bar magnets
- small objects

What to Do

1. Use a magnet to find objects that are attracted to it. List them in the boxes below:

Things Attracted to the Magnet	Things Not Attracted to the Magnet

2. How could you move a magnet without touching it?

____

____

3. Try your idea. Describe how well it works.

____

____

____

Directions: Marvin counts the money in his piggy bank. He finds that he has $1.83 in it. Think about the bills and coins that Marvin could have to total $1.83. In each box, draw a different group of bills and coins that could equal his total.

Directions: Work with a partner. Take turns rolling two number cubes. Use the chart to match your roll to a fraction. Read the fraction. Then, write a fraction that is equivalent to the one you read. Roll 10 times each. If you roll the same fraction more than once, you have to think of more than one equivalent fraction!

Roll	Fraction	Equivalent Fractions
2	$\frac{1}{4}$	
3	$\frac{2}{3}$	
4	$\frac{1}{8}$	
5	$\frac{1}{3}$	
6	$\frac{3}{8}$	
7	$\frac{5}{8}$	
8	$\frac{1}{2}$	
9	$\frac{3}{4}$	
10	$\frac{5}{6}$	
11	$\frac{2}{2}$	
12	$\frac{1}{6}$	

Spelling Activity

Write as many words as you can using the letters in each of the spelling words on page 129.

Writing Activity

Conduct some research to learn more about the sun and the moon. Add at least two facts you learned to your paragraph.

Problem-Solving Activity

Find a recipe at home or online that contains at least three fractions. Order the ingredients from least to greatest, and explain your reasoning.

Social Studies Activity

Write a fictional story about a world without rules. Include details about how the world came to have no rules and how people act in a world without rules.

Science Activity

Try moving a magnet using another magnet. What happens when you flip the magnet around? See how close the magnets need to be before one begins to move.

Critical-Thinking Activity

Ask a family member to tell you a total amount of money. Find all the ways that you can make that total with different bills and coins. Do this a few times with different amounts of money.

Directions: Read the text, and answer the questions on the next page.

The War in Space

The Rebels were fighting the Royal Guard. It was a bad war. This was probably the worst battle in 100 years. Wars used to be fought on the ground with tanks and guns. But life had moved to space. People were setting up colonies, and no one could agree on one ruler. Two groups were fighting with spacecraft. The Rebels were unhappy with the Royal Guard. They thought the Royal Guard leader was evil. The Rebels were trying to restore good in the galaxy.

These young fighters didn't even remember another type of war. They were all born in space, and their lives took place in a large spacecraft. Entire cities could live on them. The spacecraft traveled through the darkness of outer space. It was quiet in space, and things were still. It helped keep people calm so they could forget about the past. All the survivors wanted to go back to life on Earth, but it was impossible. Earth would never be the same again.

As the Rebels fought, people followed the news on the screens. They could see which fighter planes were still battling and which had come back safely. The Rebels were winning. They started to believe they had a chance after all.

The Royal Guard began to retreat. They flew away from the battle, leaving the Rebels and their supporters to celebrate. That battle was a victory! The next step was to regain control of the colonies. The Rebels wanted an honest, trusting leader. They were willing to fight to the end to make that happen.

Directions: Read "The War in Space," and then answer the questions.

1. Which is the best summary of the text?
   - (A) There is a war among students over playground space.
   - (B) A space war takes place.
   - (C) A war occurs over who travels to space first.
   - (D) Two countries fight over visiting the Space Station.

2. Who is trying to restore good for the people in space?
   - (A) the people
   - (B) the leader of the Royal Guard
   - (C) the Rebels
   - (D) the Royal Guard

3. Who could make a connection to the Rebels?
   - (A) a teacher trying to teach about historical events
   - (B) a child who wants to join a karate class
   - (C) a child is disappointed with a principal who changes the rules
   - (D) a pilot who is curious about space flight

4. Which statement about the Rebels is true?
   - (A) They are winning the fight.
   - (B) They are trying to restore good in the galaxy.
   - (C) They are fighting the Royal Guard.
   - (D) all of the above

5. What is a theme of this text?
   - (A) Be safe in space.
   - (B) Pay attention to authority, even if you disagree.
   - (C) Find a good group of people to help you.
   - (D) Fight for what you believe in.

6. What other type of text is related to this story?
   - (A) a poem about space
   - (B) a nonfiction text about a space shuttle
   - (C) a science-fiction novel about living in space in the future
   - (D) a fictional story about Earth being polluted

Directions: Write a sentence for each word. Circle the spelling word in each sentence.

Word Bank

- again
- bright
- catch
- fight
- nearly
- never
- round
- short
- sound
- would

1. ______________________________
2. ______________________________
3. ______________________________
4. ______________________________
5. ______________________________
6. ______________________________
7. ______________________________
8. ______________________________
9. ______________________________
10. ______________________________

Directions: Follow the directions.

1. Write the correct verb to complete the sentence.

   How did you ________________ after you got a shot at
   (*felt, feel, feelings*)
   the doctor's office?

2. Write the correct verb to complete the sentence.

   "Mom, did you ________________ Isaac's present yet?"
   (*wrap, wraps, wrapped*)
   Steven asked.

3. Write the plural noun to complete the sentence.

   Lily's ________________ were wiggly and about to fall out.
   (*tooth*)

4. Many plural nouns end in *–s* or *–es*. Circle the noun that does not follow this rule.

   child napkin shoe

5. Write the correct verb to complete the sentence.

   Yesterday, Ava quickly ________________ for the sleepover.
   (*pack, packs, packed*)

6. Many plural nouns end in *–s* or *–es*. Circle the noun that does not follow this rule.

   broom mouse root

Directions: Read the facts about Benjamin Franklin. Then, use the chart below to plan what you would like to include in a narrative paragraph about meeting him.

- Benjamin Franklin was a great American.
- He was able to start several companies and create four different inventions.
- Franklin did not patent any inventions because he preferred people use them for their own convenience.
- His inventions include the Franklin stove, bifocal lenses, and the lightning rod.
- Franklin was a very influential man in his time.

My Day with Benjamin Franklin

Where we met:	
What he was like:	
What we did:	

Directions: Write a narrative paragraph about meeting Benjamin Franklin. Include details about what happened when you met him. Use your notes from page 146 to help you.

Edit and Revise!

Be sure that you check your writing for:

- an introductory and concluding sentence
- sensory details that describe the experience
- correct spelling, punctuation, and capitalization

Directions: Solve each problem.

1. Record the line length.

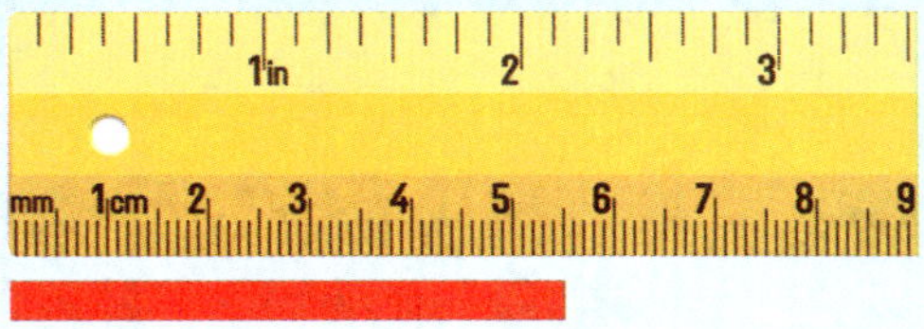

____

2. Measure the height of this page to the nearest centimeter.

____

3. Is a tulip taller or shorter than 1 meter?

____

4. Write the line length.

____

5. Is a flagpole taller or shorter than 1 meter?

____

6. Which is more likely to be taller than one yard: a person or a dog?

____

7. Write the line length.

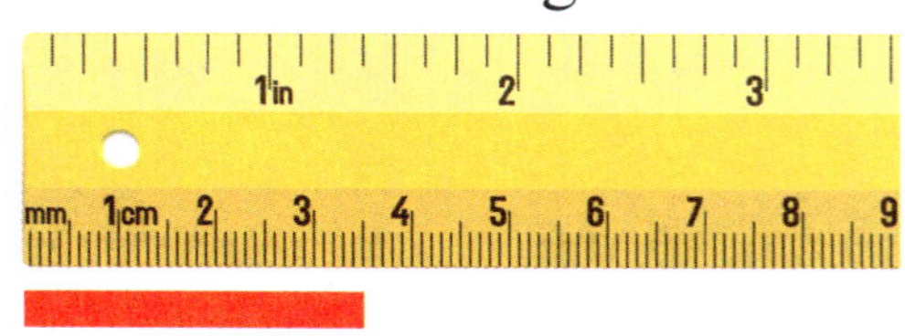

____

8. Which is longer: $1\frac{1}{2}$ yards or 45 inches?

____

Directions: Solve each problem.

1. What is the perimeter?

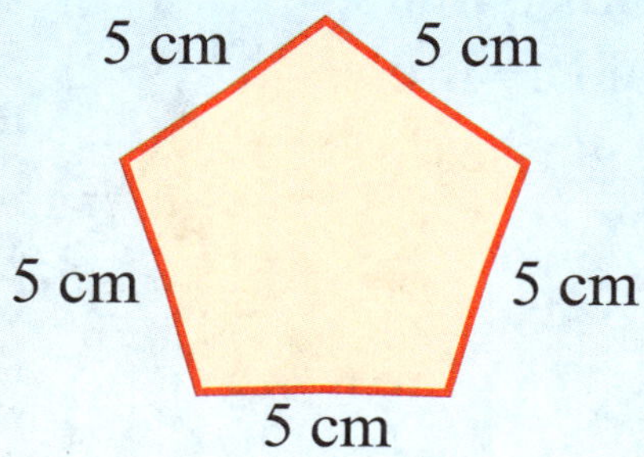

____

2. What is the perimeter?

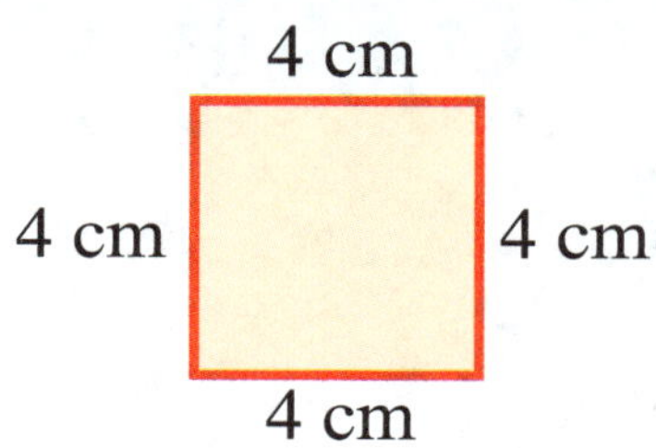

____

3. Find the perimeter of the shape below.

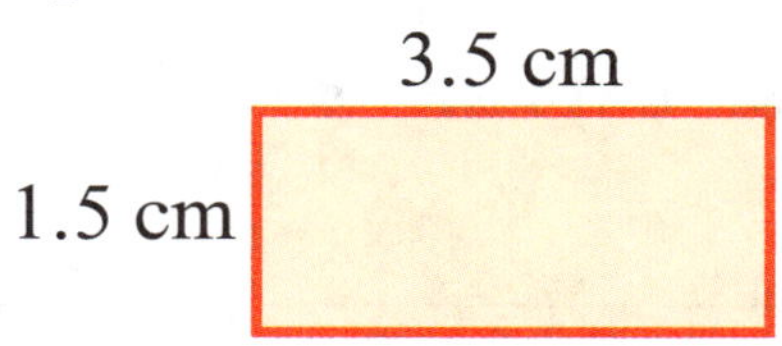

____

4. What is the perimeter of a square with 3-inch sides?

____

5. What is the perimeter of a triangle that has equal sides that measure 7 cm?

____

6. Patrick is building a rectangular planter box. One side measures 6 feet, and another side measures 4 feet. What is the perimeter of the planter box?

____

Directions: Read and solve the problem.

Anne has a pitcher of iced tea that holds 6 liters. She wants to fill 4 glasses that each hold $1\frac{1}{2}$ liters. Does Anne have enough tea to fill the glasses?

1. Draw a picture to show the problem

2. Is there enough iced tea to fill 4 glasses? Explain how you know.

____

____

____

Directions: Read and solve the problem.

The students in Mrs. Lin's third grade class voted for their favorite flavor of ice cream. The results are shown in the table. Use this information to create a bar graph.

Flavor	Number of Votes
chocolate	4
vanilla	3
strawberry	1
chocolate chip	8
cookies and cream	6

Title: ______________________________

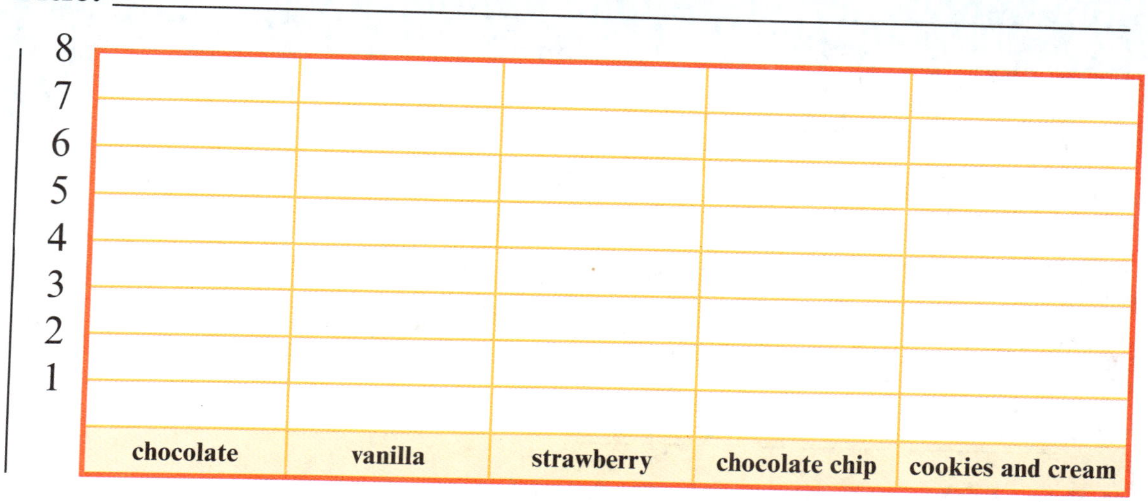

____

How many students are in Mrs. Lin's class?

____

Write and solve a question that matches the data in your graph.

____

____

____

Directions: Read the list of words in the box. These words represent democratic values. Choose three of these words, look them up, and write their definitions in your own words. Then, draw a picture to represent each word.

- liberty
- justice
- diversity
- rights
- equality
- patriotism

1. word: ____________________

____

____

____

2. word: ____________________

____

____

____

3. word: ____________________

____

____

____

Directions: Follow the steps in this experiment to discover what falls fastest.

What You Need

- sheets of paper
- large and small balls
- large and small boxes

What to Do

1. Carefully stand on a chair with the help of an adult. Drop a flat sheet of paper. Describe how it fell.

   ____

   ____

2. Scrunch another sheet of paper into a ball. Drop it. Describe how it fell.

   ____

   ____

3. Circle the object you think will fall the fastest.
   - flat paper
   - scrunched paper
   - small ball
   - large ball
   - small box
   - large box

4. Design a test to find out. Write your plan on a separate sheet of paper.

5. Conduct your test, and record your data. Be sure to think about what needs to stay the same for each object.

6. Which object fell the fastest? ______________________________

7. Which one fell the slowest? ______________________________

Directions: Every mini-grid must have each shape.
Every column must have each shape.
Every row must have each shape.

✓ X O ☆

		✓	
	☆		
			X
O			

X		☆	
✓			O

Directions: Work with a partner. Use small objects to mark your spots on the game board. Take turns rolling a number cube. Move the amount of spaces you roll. If the space has words, do what it tells you to do. The first person to the finish line wins.

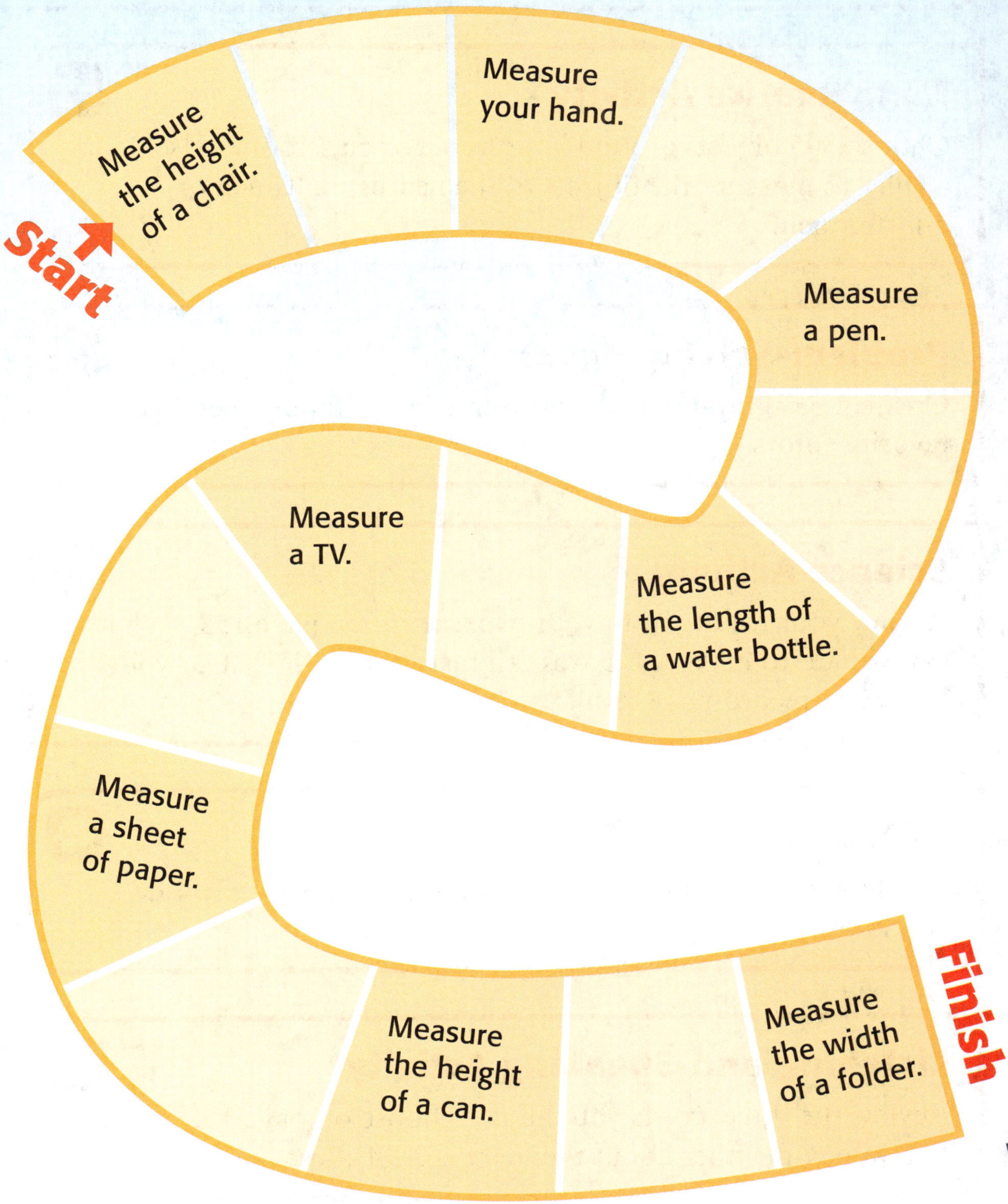

Spelling Activity

Find the words from the spelling activity on page 144 that rhyme. Write silly sentences in your best cursive handwriting. Each should use a pair of rhyming words.

Mathematics Activity

Choose 3–5 objects around your home or classroom. Use a ruler to measure the objects to the nearest half inch or quarter inch.

Problem-Solving Activity

Create a bar graph that shows each of your family member's favorite colors.

Science Activity

Review your results from your experiment on page 153. What can you do to make the boxes fall faster or slower? Test your ideas and record your results.

Critical-Thinking Activity

Create your own sudoku puzzle. Can it be solved? How do you know?

Listening-and-Speaking Activity

Review the three words you did not choose on page 152. Talk to a family member about the meanings of these words.

Answer Key

There are many open-ended pages, problems, and writing prompts in this book. For those activities, the answers will vary. Answers are only given in this answer key if they are specific.

page 7

1. B
2. D
3. C
4. B
5. A
6. C

page 8

1. C
2. D
3. B
4. A

page 10

1. "The dog has not been fed yet," my mother told us.
2. Frank yelled, "We are the state champions!"
3. 1700 Lakeview Place Springfield, OR 99810
4. *The Zookeeper's Job*
5. Addresses should include a comma between the city and state, if applicable.
6. "Bicycle Built for Two"

page 11

All circles should be checked except *Polar bear cubs are cute.*

page 13

1. 10
2. 45
3. 49
4. 60
5. 15
6. 28
7. 27
8. 32

page 14

1. 5
2. 19
3. 15
4. 24
5. 25
6. 22
7. 79
8. 14
9. 21

page 15

1. a point should be placed on 617 on the number line; 620
2. a point should be placed between 610 and 620 on the number line; 600

page 16

1. Lucy might be thinking of 195, 196, 197, 198, 199, 200, 201, 202, 203, or 204.
2. Possible answer: Using a number line is easier for me because it helps me see where the nearest ten is located.

page 18

Responses should show that warmer air outside the container cooled and condensed to form water droplets as it touched the cold container.

page 19

1. playing outside
2. top secret
3. downhill
4. eggs over easy
5. first aid
6. looking back

page 22

1. A
2. D
3. B
4. A
5. C
6. B

page 23

1. D
2. B
3. D
4. B

page 24

1. after + noon: a time of day after noon
2. air + plane: a plane that flies in the air
3. any + thing: used to describe any object
4. back + yard: a yard in the back of a house
5. birth + day: the day of one's birth
6. hair + brush: a brush for one's hair
7. stair + case: a case or a set of stairs
8. some + thing: used to describe an object
9. some + time: used to describe a time period
10. tooth + brush: a brush for one's teeth

page 25

1. quickly
2. felt
3. I will walk to school every day.
4. knowledge
5. more often
6. Sentences will vary but should include the noun *childhood*.

page 28

1. 7
2. no
3. 4
4. 6
5. Circles should be colored to show four equal groups.
6. 5
7. 4 groups of 2 pumpkins should be circled.
8. 9
9. 7
10. 6

page 29

1. seven thirty
2. 6:30
3. 
4. 
5. four forty-five
6. 7:15
7. nine fifteen
8. 

page 30

$235 + 100 + 60 + 4 = 399$; $235 + 164 = 399$

page 31

1. Possible answers: pictures, base-10 blocks, place value chart, equations; $355 + 150 = 505$; $505 - 275 = 230$
2. Possible answer: I think it's better to add the left side of the equation. Then, subtract 275 from the sum.

page 34

1. dice
2. juice
3. office
4. police
5. price
6. rice

page 37

1. C
2. B
3. A
4. C
5. C

page 38

1. A
2. B
3. A
4. B
5. D

page 39

1. drop the *e*
2. drop the *e*
3. no change
4. double the consonant
5. drop the *e*
6. sitting; double the consonant
7. depending; no change
8. making; drop the *e*
9. forgetting; double the consonant
10. taking; drop the *e*

page 40

1. lately
2. really
3. brightness
4. finding
5. bushes
6. benches
7. cries
8. dropped
9. diving
10. happily

page 43

1. 12
2. 7
3. 32
4. 4
5. –
6. 4
7. 1
8. 100, 50, 0

page 44

1. two rectangles and a square
2. pyramid
3. 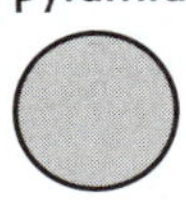
4. cylinder
5. face
6. 

page 45

$21 + 200 + 62 = 283$; $562 - 279 = 283$

page 46

1. 411; Possible strategies: regrouping, counting up, number line, base-10 blocks, pictures, equation; $740 - 329 = 411$
2. Possible answer: I like subtracting with regrouping because I can regroup 1 ten into 10 ones, then subtract the ones place.

page 47

Makes Rules: city council, Congress, teacher, principal

Enforces Rules: police officer, principal, teacher, parking enforcement, security guard

page 48

In the Northern Hemisphere, days should be getting longer between the winter solstice (mid-December) and the summer solstice (mid-June). Days should be getting shorter between the summer solstice and the winter solstice.

page 49

1. 90
2. 54
3. 7
4. 36
5. 38
6. 75

page 52

1. C
2. D
3. B
4. B

page 53

1. A
2. B
3. B
4. A
5. C

page 54

1.	above	evoba
2.	always	syawla
3.	bought	thguob
4.	himself	flesmih
5.	month	htnom
6.	should	dluohs
7.	stopped	deppots
8.	teacher	rehcaet
9.	weather	rehtaew
10.	without	tuohtiw

page 55

1. water
2. My sister never wants to share her toys with me.
3. the brown; the sandy
4. people
5. Mary
6. angrier

page 56
1. F
2. O
3. O
4. F
5. F
6. F
7. O
8. F

page 58
1. $3.77
2. $0.80
3. false
4. $0.60
5. $0.50
6. $8.70
7. $4.31
8. true
9. $2.59
10. 24

page 59
1. 80
2. 0
3. 100
4. 320
5. 30
6. 160
7. 20
8. 70
9. 90
10. 300

page 60
1. Shawn had 65 crayons. He has 38 left. Write a subtraction equation to find how much he has left; $65 - c = 38$; 27 crayons; explanations will vary
2. Kevin gave away 14 comic books. He has 62 left. Write a subtraction equation to find how many he started with;
   $b - 14 = 62$; 76 comic books; explanations will vary

page 61
1. 24 people; Possible strategies: pictures, base-10 blocks, write equations:
   $32 - 12 - 6 + 10 = 24$;
   $32 - (12 + 6) + 10 = 24$;
   $32 - 12 = 20 - 6 = 14 + 10 = 24$
2. Possible answer: I like the picture strategy because it is easy for me to see the people getting on and off the bus.

page 64

30 total squares

page 67
1. C
2. B
3. C
4. C
5. D
6. C

page 68
1. C
2. B
3. C
4. A
5. C

page 70
1. Jason's friend was trying to organize a kickball game.
2. Ted's lunch box was in the lost and found.
3. Rita's dog
4. Hector's baby brother
5. Desi's birthday party
6. Rosie's soccer uniform was mixed up with her sister's uniform.

page 73
1. 130
2. 200
3. 60
4. 800
5. 740
6. 700
7. 350
8. 400

page 74
1. 10 square units
2. 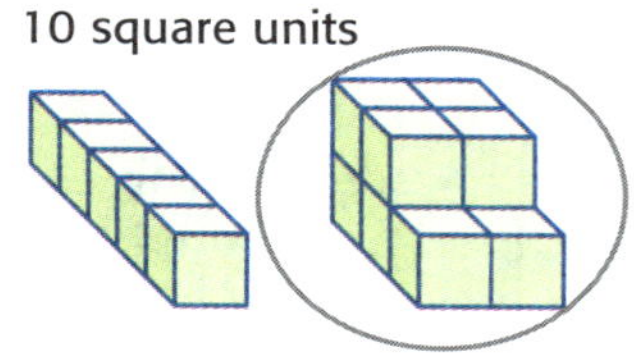
3. 12 square units
4. 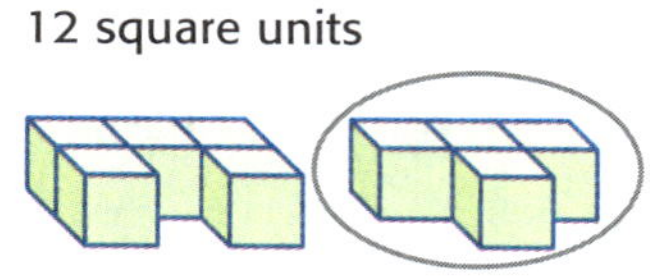
5. 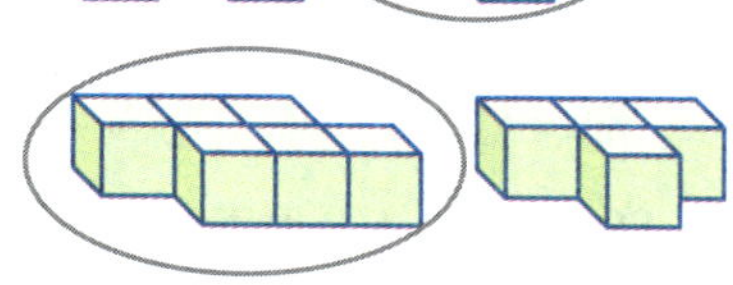
6. 8 cm^2
7. 8 cm^3
8. 9 cm^3

page 75

1. 8 breaks apart into 5 + 3; 5 × 6 = 30; 3 × 6 = 18; 30 + 18 = 48
2. 6 breaks apart into 3 + 3; 3 × 9 = 27; 3 × 9 = 27; 27 + 27 = 54

page 76

1. 8 × 9 = 72 flyers; Possible strategies: picture, repeated addition, equal groups model, array model, break apart a factor into 2 addends
2. Possible answer: I prefer to break apart one of the factors because I don't know my 8 facts yet, but I do know my 5 facts and 3 facts.

page 79

1. Colin
2. Tara
3. Tyrone
4. Lin
5. Meg
6. Ralph

page 83

1. C
2. A
3. D
4. B

page 84

1. spelling
2. largest
3. picture
4. wrong
5. children
6. heard
7. almost
8. either
9. follow
10. beside

page 85

1. lovingly; quickly
2. almost; always; happily
3. quietly; peacefully
4. quickly
5. Example: happily; warmly
6. Example: My mother greeted me joyfully after summer camp was over.

page 88

1. $32
2. 9 pages
3. 84 bananas
4. 90 minutes
5. yes
6. 12 bows

page 89

1. 96
2. 4
3. 5
4. 42
5. 60
6. ÷
7. 4
8. 3

page 90

1. Possible models: base-10 blocks, number line, picture, equal-groups model
2. 250 markers; Possible answer: I found 5 groups of 20, which is 100. Then, I found 5 groups of 30, which is 150. I added 100 and 150 to find the total, which is 250.

page 91

1. 3 × 8 = 24; 8 × 3 = 24; 24 ÷ 3 = 8; 24 ÷ 8 = 3; 4 × 6 = 24; 6 × 4 = 24; 24 ÷ 4 = 6; 24 ÷ 6 = 4; 24 × 1 = 24; 1 × 24 = 24; 24 ÷ 1 = 24; 24 ÷ 24 = 1; 2 × 12 = 24; 12 × 2 = 24; 24 ÷ 2 = 12; 24 ÷ 12 = 2
2. Pictures should show one fact family.

page 94

Kay and Josh's Message: Come to my house to play.

page 98

1. A
2. B
3. D
4. B
5. B
6. D

page 99

1. aunt; tnua
2. brother; rehtorb
3. daughter; rethguad
4. father; rehtaf
5. grandfather; rehtafdnarg
6. grandmother; rehtomdnarg
7. mother; rehtom
8. sister; retsis
9. son; nos
10. uncle; elcnu

page 103

1. 6 liters
2. 3
3. 4
4. 800 mL
5. The book should be circled.
6. less
7. The box labeled *Ally's toys* should be circled.

page 104

1.

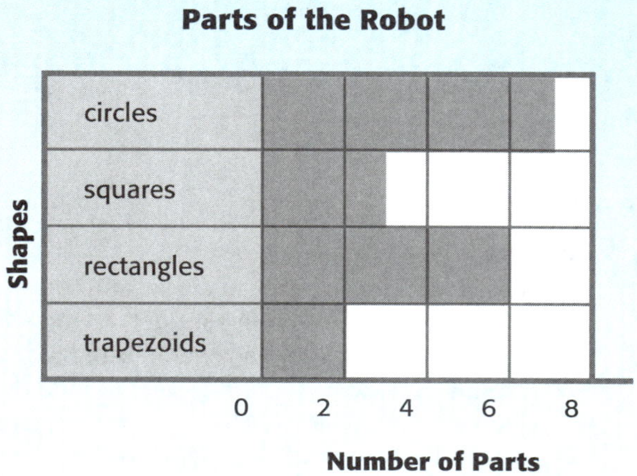

2.

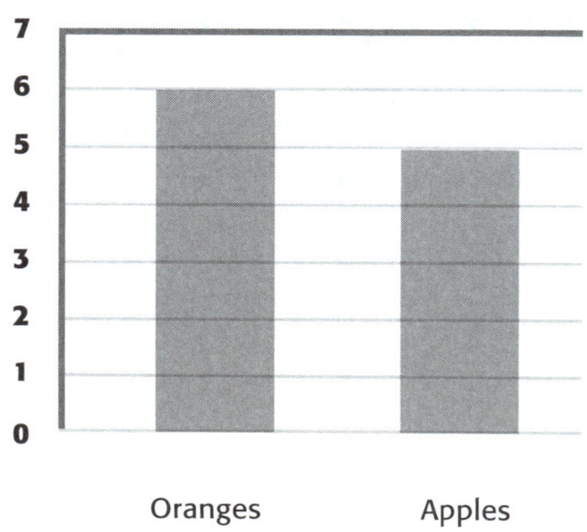

3. 25; 15

page 105

1. 36 pieces of pie; $6 \times 6 = 36$; Possible picture:

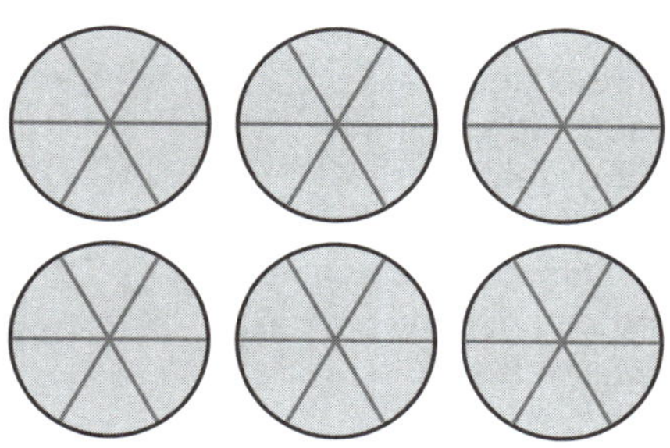

2. 4 pieces of pie; Possible explanation: There are 36 total pieces. Since 9 people will share them, each person will get 4 pieces of pie.

page 106

1. \$182; $7 \times 10 = 70$, $70 + 112 = 182$

2. No; Julie has \$182. The bike costs \$225. Julie needs an additional \$43 to buy the bike.

page 109

1. 5
2. 10
3. 25
4. 75
5. 25
6. 5

page 113

1. B
2. B
3. B
4. D
5. C

page 114

1. forgot
2. sorry
3. already
4. below
5. desert
6. might
7. study
8. which
9. tonight
10. nothing

page 115

1. stomping along
2. the beautiful forest
3. baseball championship
4. song titles
5. uncle john's farm
6. titles of poems

page 118

1. 63
2. 35 hats
3. 16 ears
4. Arrays may have 7 rows and 8 columns or 8 rows and 7 columns.
5. Arrays should have 6 rows and 1 column.
6. 40

page 119

1. Check that the sections have about the same area. Possible model:

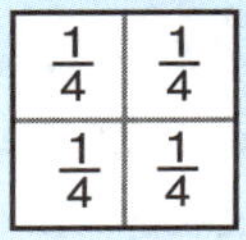

2. Check that the sections have about the same area. Possible model:

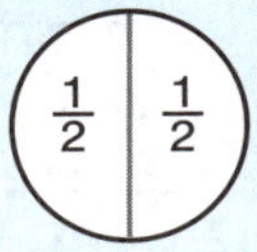

3. Check that the sections have about the same area. Possible model:

$\frac{2}{3}$ 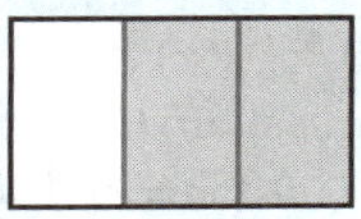

4. $\frac{3}{6}$ or $\frac{1}{2}$
5. $\frac{2}{3}$
6. $\frac{1}{2}$
7. Check that the sections have about the same area. The listed fraction should match what is shaded.

page 120

1. Possible model:

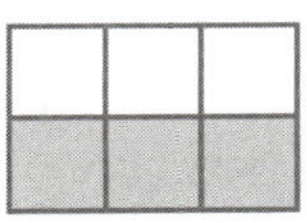

2. Yes, Destiny is correct. Since her family ate 3 of the 6 pieces, they ate $\frac{1}{2}$ of the cake.

page 121

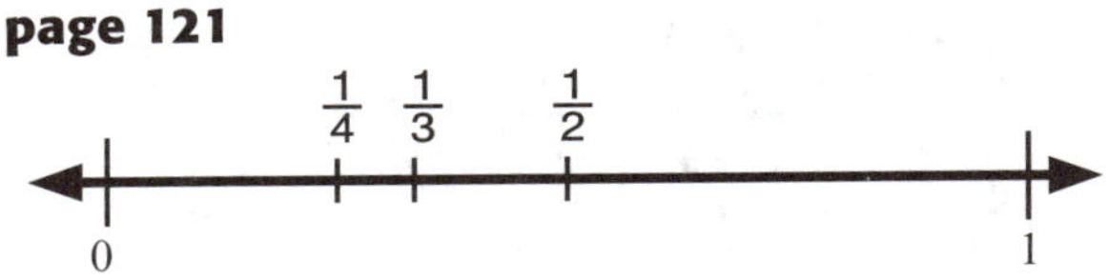

1. $\frac{1}{4}$
2. $\frac{1}{2}$
3. Possible explanation: I put $\frac{1}{2}$ in the middle of 0 and 1. Then, I thought about dividing the number line into fourths and found $\frac{1}{4}$. Lastly, I know that $\frac{1}{3}$ is greater than $\frac{1}{4}$, but less than $\frac{1}{2}$, so I put $\frac{1}{3}$ between $\frac{1}{4}$ and $\frac{1}{2}$.

page 128

1. C
2. D
3. D
4. A
5. A
6. B

page 130

1. New York, NY
2. Oklahoma City, OK
3. Chicago, IL
4. Jacksonville, FL
5. Check for commas between the city and state, if applicable.

page 133

1. $\frac{1}{2}$
2. $\frac{4}{6}$
3. $\frac{1}{2}$ or other equivalent fraction
4. $\frac{2}{3}$ or other equivalent fraction
5. $\frac{1}{4}$
6. $\frac{1}{2}$ or other equivalent fraction
7. $\frac{1}{3}$ or other equivalent fraction
8. $\frac{6}{16}$ or other equivalent fraction
9. $\frac{5}{6}$ or other equivalent fraction
10. Answers will vary. Examples: $\frac{3}{6}$, $\frac{5}{10}$, $\frac{4}{8}$

page 134

1. 18, 180
2. 20, 200
3. 27, 270
4. 8, 80
5. 15, 150
6. 28, 280
7. 14, 140
8. 81, 810

page 135

1. Possible model:

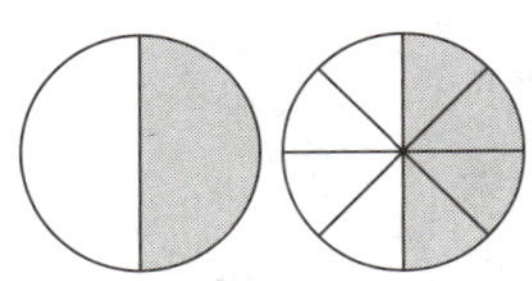

1. Possible answer: I disagree with Max. Joey and Max ate the same amount because $\frac{1}{2} = \frac{4}{8}$.
2. $\frac{4}{8}$; Since Max ate $\frac{4}{8}$, or $\frac{1}{2}$, of the pizza, he has $\frac{4}{8}$ or $\frac{1}{2}$ of the pizza left.

page 136

1. Possible model:

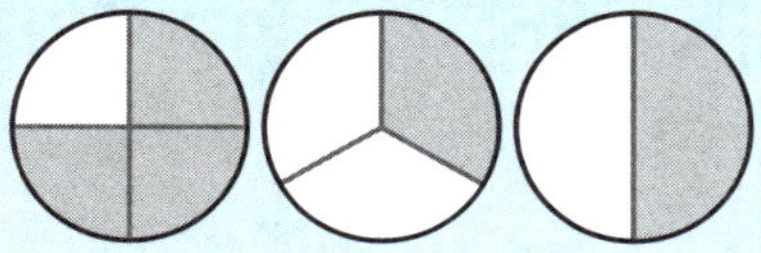

2. $\frac{1}{3}$, $\frac{1}{2}$, $\frac{3}{4}$; Possible answer: I drew a model for each fraction and compared the parts shaded to order them from least to greatest.

page 143

1. B
2. C
3. C
4. D
5. D
6. C

page 145

1. feel
2. wrap
3. teeth
4. child
5. packed
6. mouse

page 148

1. $5\frac{1}{2}$ cm or 55 mm
2. 28 cm
3. shorter
4. 3 in.
5. taller
6. a person
7. $3\frac{1}{2}$ cm or 35 mm
8. $1\frac{1}{2}$ yards

page 149

1. 25 cm
2. 16 cm
3. 10 cm
4. 12 in.
5. 21 cm
6. 20 ft.

page 150

1. Possible models: fraction model, picture, number line
2. Yes, the four glasses together hold 6 liters because 4 groups of $1\frac{1}{2}$ is 6.

page 151

Favorite Ice Cream Flavor

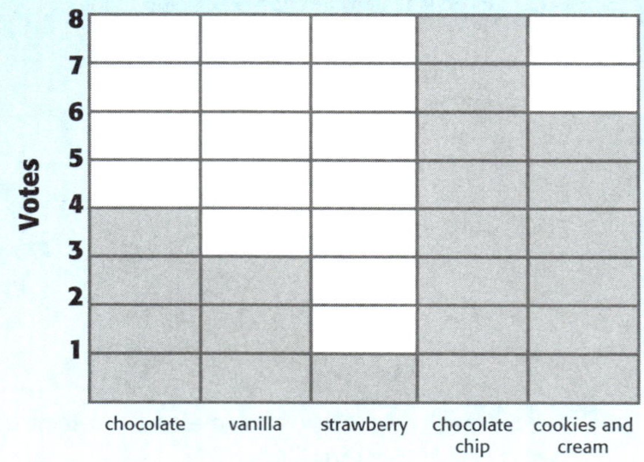

1. 22 students; $4 + 3 + 1 + 8 + 6 = 22$
2. Possible question: How many more students voted for chocolate and chocolate chip than strawberry and cookies and cream?; 5 students; $12 - 7 = 5$

page 154

X	O	✓	☆
✓	☆	X	O
☆	✓	O	X
O	X	☆	✓

X	O	☆	✓
☆	✓	O	X
✓	☆	X	O
O	X	✓	☆

Skills and Standards in This Book

Today's standards have created more consistency in how mathematics and English language arts are taught. In the past, states and school districts had their own standards for each grade level. However, what was taught in a specific grade in one location may have been taught in a different grade in another location. This made it difficult when students moved.

Today, many states and school districts have adopted new standards. This means that for the first time, there is greater consistency in what is being taught at each grade level, with the ultimate goal of getting students ready to be successful in college and in their careers.

Standards Features

The overall goal for the standards is to better prepare students for life. Today's standards have several key features:

- They describe what students should know and be able to do at each grade level.
- They are rigorous and dive deeply into the content.
- They require higher-level thinking and analysis.
- They require students to explain and justify answers.
- They are aimed at making sure students are prepared for college and/or their future careers.

Unit Outline

This book is designed to help your child meet today's rigorous standards. This section describes the standards-based skills covered in each unit of study.

Unit 1	• Read and answer questions about a narrative and a piece of nonfiction text. • Practice reading and writing spelling words. • Use correct punctuation and capitalization. • Write an informative paragraph about animals in the tundra.	• Multiply, add, and subtract within 100. • Round to the nearest 10 and 100. • Identify the purpose of rules. • Observe condensation on a cold container.
Unit 2	• Read and answer questions about a narrative and a piece of nonfiction text. • Practice reading and writing spelling words. • Identify and use nouns, adverbs, and verb tenses. • Write an opinion paragraph about a season. • Interpret products as equal groups.	• Tell time to the nearest minute. • Use strategies to add and subtract large numbers. • Identify ways to volunteer. • Identify the composition of soil.
Unit 3	• Read and answer questions about a narrative and a piece of nonfiction text. • Practice reading and writing spelling words. • Identify spelling generalizations. • Write a narrative about a holiday. • Fluently add, subtract, and multiply.	• Identify attributes of shapes. • Identify people who make and enforce rules. • Observe a pattern in sunrise and sunset times.
Unit 4	• Read and answer questions about a narrative and a piece of nonfiction text. • Practice reading and writing spelling words. • Identify and use nouns, pronouns, and adjectives. • Write an informative paragraph about earthquakes. • Add and subtract amounts of money.	• Multiply numbers by multiples of 10. • Solve two- and three-step word problems. • Understand why laws are important. • Observe seeds growing into plants.
Unit 5	• Read and answer questions about a narrative and a piece of nonfiction text. • Practice reading and writing spelling words. • Form and use possessives. • Write an opinion paragraph about an animal. • Round numbers to the nearest 10 and 100.	• Calculate volume and area. • Use strategies to multiply. • Read and analyze the First Amendment. • Observe the bones in a human hand.

Unit 6	• Read and answer questions about a narrative. • Practice reading and writing spelling words. • Identify and use adverbs. • Write a narrative about land travel.	• Solve multiplication word problems. • Use strategies to multiply and divide within 100. • Draw a map of a city. • Identify conductors.
Unit 7	• Read and answer questions about a piece of nonfiction text. • Practice reading and writing spelling words. • Identify and use nouns, adjectives, and adverbs. • Write an informative paragraph about sharks.	• Estimate and compare mass and liquid volumes. • Create and interpret charts and bar graphs. • Use strategies to multiply and divide. • Research another country. • Test the acidity of local water.
Unit 8	• Read and answer questions about narrative. • Practice reading and writing spelling words. • Use correct capitalization. • Write an opinion paragraph about ice cream. • Identify products as equal groups.	• Partition shapes into equal parts. • Understand fractions as parts of wholes. • Represent fractions on a number line. • Identify qualities of a good leader. • Identify what affects how far objects roll.
Unit 9	• Read and answer questions about a piece of nonfiction text. • Practice reading and writing spelling words. • Use commas in addresses. • Write an informative paragraph about the sun and the moon.	• Identify equivalent fractions. • Multiply numbers by multiples of 10. • Compare fractions in word problems. • Identify the purpose of rules in different settings. • Identify magnetic objects.
Unit 10	• Read and answer questions about a narrative. • Practice reading and writing spelling words. • Correctly use verb tenses and irregular plural nouns. • Write a narrative about meeting Benjamin Franklin. • Estimate and measure lengths of objects.	• Calculate perimeters of objects. • Solve fraction word problems. • Create and interpret bar graphs. • Define democratic values. • Design an experiment to determine how objects fall.

Congratulations

_______________________________________!

(name)

You have completed
Conquering Third Grade!

presented on ____________________
(date)